D1450958

THE NILE AND ANCIENT EGYPT

The tale of human habitation of the Nile Valley is a long one; it includes famine, disaster, global environmental events and human resolve told against a background of ever-changing landscape. In this volume, Judith Bunbury examines the region over a 10,000-year period, from the Neolithic to the Roman conquest. Charting the progression of the river as it meanders through the region and over the ages, she demonstrates how ancient Egyptians attempted to harness the Nile's power as a force for good. Over the generations, they learned how to farm and build on its banks, and also found innovative solutions to cope in a constantly evolving habitat. Using the latest theories and evidence, this richly illustrated volume also provides a blueprint for the future management of the Nile.

Judith Bunbury is Senior Tutor at St Edmund's College, Teaching Associate in the Department of Earth Sciences and member of the MacDonald Research Institute at the University of Cambridge. She has worked on several major sites in Egypt, including the temples at Karnak and the Giza pyramids.

THE NILE AND ANCIENT EGYPT

Changing Land- and Waterscapes, from the Neolithic to the Roman Era

JUDITH BUNBURY

Cambridge University

CAMBRIDGE
UNIVERSITY PRESS

CAMBRIDGE
UNIVERSITY PRESS

University Printing House, Cambridge CB2 8BS, United Kingdom

One Liberty Plaza, 20th Floor, New York, NY 10006, USA

477 Williamstown Road, Port Melbourne, VIC 3207, Australia

314–321, 3rd Floor, Plot 3, Splendor Forum, Jasola District Centre,
New Delhi – 110025, India

79 Anson Road, #06-04/06, Singapore 079906

Cambridge University Press is part of the University of Cambridge.

It furthers the University's mission by disseminating knowledge in the pursuit of
education, learning, and research at the highest international levels of excellence.

www.cambridge.org
Information on this title: www.cambridge.org/9781107012158
DOI: 10.1017/9780511997884

First published 2019

Printed in the United Kingdom by TJ International Ltd. Padstow Cornwall

A catalogue record for this publication is available from the British Library.

Library of Congress Cataloging-in-Publication Data
Names: Bunbury, J. (Judith), author.
Title: The Nile and Ancient Egypt : changing land- and waterscapes,
from the Neolithic to the Roman Era / Judith Bunbury.
Description: Cambridge, United Kingdom; New York, NY:
Cambridge University Press, [2019] | Includes bibliographical references and index.
Identifiers: LCCN 2019000697 | ISBN 9781107012158 (hardback)
Subjects: LCSH: Nile River – History. | Water-supply – Nile River
Watershed – Management – History. | Water resources development –
Nile River – History – To 1500. | Climatic changes – Social aspects –
Nile River Valley – History – To 1500. | Agriculture – Nile River Valley.
Classification: LCC DT116.B86 2019 | DDC 932–dc23
LC record available at https://lccn.loc.gov/2019000697

ISBN 978-1-107-01215-8 Hardback

For Alan Smith who said this should be a book

CONTENTS

FIGURES

TABLES

ACKNOWLEDGEMENTS

The ideas and case studies compiled here accumulated over twenty-five years of fieldwork in Egypt, much of it with Angus Graham of Uppsala University, who also supplied a number of the images. During that time many archaeologists and workmen in Egypt have honed and challenged our ideas. I would like to thank a representative group here: Maha Mansourt at the Library of Alexandria for sharing the wonderful digital resources that are being collected there; members of the International Association of Landscape Archaeologists (IALA) for their inspiration as I was developing my ideas; my masters and doctoral students for their energetic work and generosity in sharing ideas on a large number of the projects, including Tom Branton, Taryn Duckworth, David Dufton, Erin Earl, Pedro Gonçalves, Ellie Hughes, Katy Lutley, Ben Pennington, Laurence Pryer, Ying Qin and Graham Smith.

I would also like to thank my many colleagues who have invited us to their excavations and tirelessly explained the archaeological niceties of the sites, particularly difficult in the case of an ignorant geologist. These heroes include Ian Shaw, who first decided that a geologist would be useful in Egypt, Sally-Ann Ashton, Bettina Bader, James Barrett, Liz Bloxham, Dan Boatright, Janine Bourieau, Tom Branton, Betsy Bryan, Alan Clapham, John Cooper, Vivian Davies, Mostafa Elwakeel, Mario Fabrizio, Omer Farouk, Lalla Farouk, Ignatio Fiz, Charly French, Renée Friedmann, Ann-Cathrin Gabel, Alison Gascoigne, Aude Grazer-Ohara, Darcy Hackley, Mohammed Hamdan, Hanan Hassan, Irmgard Hein, Jay Heidel, Ian Hodder, Anna Kathrin Hodgkinson, Morag Hunter, Ahmed Hussein, Salima Ikram, Jean Jacquet, Helen Jacquet-Gordon, Rob Jamieson, David Jeffreys, Ray Johnson, Liz Jones, Mohsen Kamel, David Kennedy, Ayman Koko, Mark Lehner, Veerla Linseele, Piers Litherland, Myrto Malouta, Silvie Marchand, Geoffrey Martin, Aurélia Masson-Berghof, Liam McNamara, Marie Millett, Wim van Neer, Paul Nicholson, Ian Ostericher, Sarah Parcak, Virpi Perunkaa, Jan Picton, Pam Rose, Ilona Regulski, Joanne Rowland, Prof Sciuti, Graham

Smith, Lawrence Smith, Kate Spence, Neal Spencer, Alice Stevens, Steven Stoddard, Jo Story, Kris Strutt, Eva Subias, Geoffrey Tassie, Ana Tavares, Leslie Warden, Nicholas Warner and Penny Wilson. The more candid of them have told me how much they fear my endless questions, especially those about the tiny 'mouse poo'-sized grains of pottery that have told us so much! The errors of understanding in this book remain my own.

Thanks must also go to the many inspectors of antiquities in Egypt who have assisted our work as well as to the ministers and secretaries of the Ministry of Antiquities/Supreme Council of Antiquities, under whose aegis permission was granted. Particular supporters include Mr Mansour Boraik and Mr Suleyman Ibrahim in Luxor. Our work has continued through the generosity of the Egypt Exploration Society, the British Academy, the British Museum, the Gurob Harem Palace Project, the Friends of Nekhen, Ancient Egypt Research Associates, New Kingdom Research Foundation, Centre National des Récherches Scientifiques, Metropolitan Museum, American University in Cairo and Cambridge University. I am also much indebted to my family for their practical support and to the Farouk family of Luxor who have provided logistical infrastructure and many cups of tea.

Since no book project can continue without the encouragement of its editors, I extend my thanks to Beatrice Rehl, Reim Rowe and the reviewers for steering me so deftly through the process.

INTRODUCTION

The Nile, forever new and old,
Among the living and the dead,
Its mighty, mystic stream has rolled.

Henry Wadsworth Longfellow
(1807–82)

M Y ENTHUSIASM FOR THE NILE BEGAN AS AN EAGER POST-graduate many years ago and has grown over countless excursions and excavations in Egypt. Observation of the geology of the landscape naturally led me to wonder what part humans have played in the river's life over millennia or, perhaps more accurately, the role of the Nile in defining the progress and development of the peoples who lived by and depended upon it. Has the Nile existed as it appears to us today or has it changed? What are the key influences on the Nile and how does this mighty river react? How have the inhabitants of the Nile Valley learnt to adapt to their environment? How are they able to harness the power of the Nile to their advantage and still live in harmony with it?

The ancient Egyptian kingdoms at their greatest extent stretched more than 2,000 kilometres up the Nile and included diverse habitats. In the north, they included the Mediterranean coast and the delta, while further south the thread of cultivation along the Nile Valley passed through the vast desert of the Sahara. As global climate and landscapes changed and evolved, the habitable parts of the kingdoms shifted. Modern studies suggest that episodes of desertification and greening swept across Egypt over periods of 1,000 years. In order to present a narrative of landscape and climate change in Egypt, I have explored the changes to the desert, the Nile Valley with its fringing wadis and the Northern Delta. Rather than isolated events, the changes in Egypt are characterised by a constant shift of events, so although broadly historic, this narrative follows a series of habitats as they change and evolve through time.

HUMANS AND CLIMATE CHANGE: HOW PAST PEOPLES CAN INFORM OUR RESPONSES TO LANDSCAPE AND CLIMATE CHANGE

E GYPT, PART OF THE CRADLE OF CIVILISATION, IS A PRODUCT OF the Nile, the world's longest river. Since the majority of the country is desert, its people live mainly along the Nile on the fertile floodplain and delta of the river. The population of Egypt, both now and in the past, has been subject to the river's behaviour and geography and the Nile Valley and Saharan region were important routes out of Africa for hominids in the early prehistoric period, who radiated from the Rift Valley.

To give a flavour of the persistence of habitation in this area, we need to consider the time before the last ice age, around 30,000 BC, when permanent populations were already present in Egypt. Evidence remains of extensive deposits of stone tools and workshops around the Faiyum and Kharga oases. We know from redeposited tools that they made use of habitats in the Nile Valley but subsequent river activity has destroyed traces of this period of human activity.

During the glaciations of the last ice age (c. 110,000 to 9640 BC), as global temperatures dropped, the Sahara became arid and inhospitable. At the same time, the Nile shrank and became more approachable as its water supply from the Ethiopian Monsoon dwindled. At the poles, cooler temperatures meant that water was locked away in the ice caps, lowering global sea level and consequently reducing the water level in the Mediterranean. The Nile, eroding down to the new sea level, formed narrow canyons, shrinking the habitable area of Egypt considerably.

These glacial processes were reversed during the interglacials, with the reinvigoration of the Ethiopian Monsoon and rising sea level. The delta was flooded as the sea rose and fresh water was held back in the Nile Valley, which became wet and marshy. These marshes, liable to flooding and inhabited by hippos and other large mammals, were a rich, if dangerous, habitat. Upstream, the rising Nile also extended its floodplain and, in places, overflowed into the Sahara, creating a patchwork of lakes that formed an almost perfect habitat for early humans and ushered in the Holocene, the time since around 11,000 years ago. In the lake-shore environments there was access to fresh water, fish, game and, as lakes receded during dryer times, calorie-rich grains.

Throughout history, climate oscillations caused the Nile to rise and fall as well as periodically drying and re-wetting the Nile margins and the Saharan lake beds. In the wetter times, the Nile, as all rivers do, responded to the rise by rebuilding its delta and floodplain and developing into a meandering river. As the meandering river matured, the inhabitants of Egypt became increasingly dependent upon the Nile as the deserts dried. They left the deserts and migrated into the oases and to the Nile Valley flanks. With time, the Nile coalesced into fewer channels and humans came even closer to the river.

Closer proximity meant that the Nile-dwellers began to understand how the Nile swelled and diminished through its annual cycle and also how the channels and islands behaved over the generations. This emerging knowledge was captured in myths, ceremonies and agricultural practices as well as in the more empirical calendars and Nilometer records. Record keeping particularly was developed to aid the collection of taxes since knowledge of the size of land packages and the depth of the flood allowed the state to calculate the likely agricultural yield. With growing expertise, an increasing number of practices designed to manage and control the Nile flood developed and accreted. In modern times, with the construction of the Aswan Dam, the Nile level can be held steady throughout the year, maximising the potential for transport and irrigation although simultaneously, as we will see, creating problems of salination and water supply.

Geological Origins of the Egyptian Landscape

The geological canvas upon which this history of the Nile Valley is placed is one of extreme variation. Full details appear in Said (1981) and are excellently summarised by Sampsell (2014) but, in brief, the rocks of most of Egypt are a stack of more or less flat-lying, sedimentary deposits resting upon an ancient crystalline basement. At the base of the sediments lie the important aquifers of the Nubian sandstone and above this a stack of chalk and limestone rocks. These were laid down during the geological era of the Cretaceous, around 70 million years ago, in a warm shallow sea. During ice ages, when the water level was low in the Mediterranean basin, the Nile cut down through this sandwich of sediments to form a deep canyon with tributary canyons, similar in size to the Grand Canyon. This canyon stretched from Aswan in the south to the Mediterranean, or rather the salty and dried-up remains of what was left of it, in the north.

Although the Nile currently has no tributaries in Egypt, in the distant past, when the sea level was much lower than today and there was more rain locally, the tributary river valleys were deeply incised into the walls of the canyon through which the Nile flowed (Said et al. 1962, 1981). Later, when sea levels rose, these valleys became inactive and were choked with sand and gravel from the desert to become the wadis. In the Eastern Desert, these wadis continue to host drought-tolerant plants and fauna as well as the local tribes, creating additional habitable land beyond the Nile Valley (Hobbs 1990). Although rains are rare, perhaps once in ten years, they can cause flash floods, the wadi gravels become fluidised and collapse, carrying gravel, roads and other material with them.

While the wadis form mainly in the flanks of the Nile Valley, to the north in the delta, as sediment was eroded away, mounds of sand were left between the branches of the delta's distributary system. The relict mounds still emerge from the Nile floodplain in the north of Egypt today; they are known as the gezirehs. With rising sea levels, the old river valleys refilled and a thin veneer, around 10–20 m thick, of rich, black mud was deposited on top of the gravels and around the gezirehs. It is this thin layer of mud upon which the majority of the modern inhabitants of Egypt rely for agriculture and from which they derived the early name for Egypt, *kmt*, the black land. The sandy mounds of the gezirehs became some of the earliest inhabited parts of the delta.

Landscape and Early Egyptology

Our understanding of the landscape processes was slow to develop. The earliest excavations in Egypt were preoccupied with the exploration and deciphering of the hieroglyphs that were visible on the monuments (Thompson 2015). These monuments, known throughout the world, have long been a subject of scholarship and many ancient visitors recorded their wonder at the achievements of the past in their inscriptions. Modern Egyptology began to gather momentum in the late eighteenth century. In 1798 Napoleon, as part of his campaign to add Egypt to his empire, landed a force of 160 scholars alongside the army to collate and propagate knowledge. The 'savants', as they were known, published newspapers and made maps, plans and drawings of monuments, landscapes, plants and animals. A comprehensive catalogue of Egypt emerged, including many images of monuments and their inscriptions so detailed and accurate that, although hieroglyphs had not been deciphered at the time, the images could later be used to translate texts that subsequently disappeared. The process of recording was interrupted when the British army arrived and the French army withdrew. The savants left with as many of their notes and artefacts as they could. They even had a copy of the Rosetta Stone that later proved to be the key to deciphering hieroglyphs, although the original had been taken into custody by the British army.

Back in France, the savants' work was collated into spectacular display volumes with many plates, today known as *Le Déscription de L'Égypte*. Perhaps somewhat nettled after their departure from Egypt, French scholars, including Jean-François Champollion, continued to compete with other European scholars to be first to decipher the meaning of the hieroglyphs. Success was slow in coming but by the time of his death in 1832, Champollion and his competitors were making good progress and were anxious for new samples of text to extend their understanding. To obtain these texts, scholars travelled through Egypt copying inscriptions and, as the mania developed, excavating the ancient ruins to find more. Egyptology continued to be focussed on the recovery and preservation of texts until Flinders Petrie (1853–1942), a trained surveyor, started his work in 1880.

Few records of the archaeological context in which the texts appeared were kept until the late nineteenth century when Joseph Hekekyan Bey (1807–75) (Jeffreys 2010) and Petrie, among others, began to make detailed observations of the find spots. Modern archaeology now takes careful note of the 'context' or sediments in which inscriptions are found, yielding valuable information about the ancient landscape. Perhaps unsurprisingly, given the absence of context for many of the texts, translations of the texts and interpretations of the sites took it for granted that the landscape in which the sites were set had been much as it is now. When Baines and Malek (1980) compiled their atlas of ancient Egypt, they realised that, as there was so little information about how the Nile moved, they were obliged to portray it in its modern course, regardless of the period and the ancient geography.

Gertrude Caton-Thompson in the early twentieth century suggested that the environment had not always been what it is today. The geologist in her team, Elinor Gardner, observed from sediments associated with the ruins that they had been built in wetter times. Soon afterwards, during the 1960s, there was a major campaign of rescue archaeology preceding the inundation of a large part of Nubia with the waters of the reservoir, Lake Nasser. From these surveys, further prehistoric discoveries were made, including those by Fred Wendorf and Romuald Schild at Nabta Playa (1998). Observations of the sediments associated with these sites made it clear that the environment was a crucial consideration in the occupation patterns of prehistoric humans. From their excavations, Wendorf and Schild could see how strategic lakeshore sites were reoccupied, even though the traces of earlier occupation were shallowly buried and no longer visible. Furthermore, ancient sand dunes buried in the lake mud had contained reservoirs of fresh water.

Manfred Bietak, who also participated in the Aswan Dam rescue excavations, later went on to explore the large sites of Tell El-Dab'a and Piramesse in the delta, taking due account of the waterways that had surrounded and connected the sites. Around the same time Karl Butzer, working in the Nile Valley at the Pyramids of Giza, started to apply the evidence from sediments around historic sites to understanding their environment. His seminal work on the Nile Valley, 'Early Hydraulic Civilization in Egypt: A Study in Cultural Ecology' (1976), set the scene for modern archaeological investigations where sediment logs and boreholes are considered a routine part of the work.

To sample the sediment, a narrow column of around 10 cm in diameter is extracted using an auger. This is a barrel at the end of a long rod that cuts and lifts around 5–10 cm depth of sediment from a known depth for subsequent analysis, including description of the type of sediment and the archaeological and other remains encapsulated in it. More detail of this process is given in the Appendix. Broadly, the results of auger analysis yield a detailed history of that point in space which may go back thousands of years. Fragments of pottery, bone, textile and building and decorative stones can be compared with the neighbouring sites from which they are derived to determine the type of activity and sometimes the date that the sediment was deposited. At the same time the sediment description reveals the source of the material, whether from the Nile or the desert, and the speed of the current that delivered it. For example, a harbour will accumulate anoxic, smelly mud while the main riverbank will accumulate coarse sand and pebbles. A set of auger cores, when combined with other geographical data, reveals the history of the whole landscape.

This type of investigation was taken up by others, who were augmented by the parallel explorations of Attia (1954) and his teams on behalf of the Geological Survey of Egypt. Similarly, Stanley and Warne (1994) used carbon dates and more than a hundred boreholes to explore the architecture of the delta. Around the same time David Jeffreys added a programme of auger coring to the work of the Survey of Memphis. Over the ensuing thirty years his team cored and logged at hundreds of locations, totalling more than 2 km of sediment. As they went, they trained a battalion of students in the art of logging and landscape interpretation. In this book, we draw upon the work of these students and others who have investigated numerous sites across Egypt: in the Nile floodplain, in the delta and in the deserts. To hundreds of boreholes from tens of sites they have added emerging techniques to their interpretation, drawing upon satellite imagery and geophysics to enhance their understanding of the changing landscape through Egyptian prehistory and history and fathom the patterns of human habitation through antiquity.

The Nile as a large river system, forced by climate change, responds according to the laws of physics, as any large river does. The borehole investigations reveal that although early humans tracked habitats as the landscape changed, with time they started to understand the river and its behaviour, and intervene, adapting it to their own needs for transport, drinking water, food and irrigation.

Notes on Dating

In this exploration of the history of landscape change, I have used the traditional nomenclature for the periods of Egyptian history. Although dates for the Egyptian periods are quite well understood, there is naturally some variation in the years assigned to the reigns of the kings, particularly for those who reigned three or four thousand years ago. Egyptian artefacts are generally dated either from inscriptions or from pottery series dates. Pottery chronology dating, pioneered by Petrie during his excavations in the late nineteenth and early twentieth century, relied upon the ancient Egyptian taste for fashion and novelty in pottery. Initially, Petrie identified a series of developments in pottery from a Pre-Dynastic cemetery that he was excavating at Naqada in the Luxor area. Since then, pottery specialists, whose work has been essential to the development of the narrative presented in this book, have extended our understanding of pottery types to include all archaeological time since the earliest known sherds from Egypt discovered by Wendorf at Wadi Bakht through the Islamic period to the present day. In the same way that Emma Bridgewater's ceramics will endure as the look for the 2000s, ancient pottery can sometimes be dated to a specific king's reign or, in some cases, even to a subdivision of the reign.

The pottery dates are also tied to the ancient Egyptian king lists. Initially created as a historical record of the origins and hence legitimacy of the kings, these lists were later compiled by Manetho, a priest and scholar of the early third century BC, to create a calendar for ancient Egypt. Manetho tended to arrange the kings in a chronological series, assuming that none overlapped with any other. However, modern scholars increasingly consider that some kings continued to reign (or claim to reign) while others were also reigning. Understandably, the degree of overlap was not generally made explicit, since they potentially had rival claims to the throne or may have been de facto rulers of separate geographical areas.

However, within the king lists, individual kings and their subjects or correspondents were often punctilious in recording the precise year of the reign in which they were founding a temple, recording a battle, making a gift or writing a letter. For example, at the Palace of Malkata, near Luxor, many labels recording details of gifts to Amenhotep III on the occasion of the thirty-fourth jubilee of his reign were recovered from the desert around the ruined buildings. Some sources even include, as do our modern dates, the month, the day and the season as well as the year of the reign and the identity of the king. Synchronisation of these king lists and regnal year dates with celestial phenomena described in the texts provides even greater precision to the timescale that in this work is then expressed as a year BC or AD.

Where pottery or regnal year dates are not available, the somewhat blunter instrument of carbon dating may be employed to assign an approximate date to a deposit. Initially, carbon dating was thought to be extremely accurate. However, comparison with wood of known age collected from Egypt among other places showed that the dates could only be determined to an accuracy of +/− 100 years and that there were small-scale variations recorded in tree rings that were part of the discrepancy. Comparison with analyses of tree rings from long-lived species to correct the carbon dates improved the accuracy to around +/− 50 years. Modern laboratory processes continue to be refined and improved.

Additionally, in 1950 the first nuclear tests changed the carbon isotope composition of the atmosphere and biosphere forever, so carbon dates are quoted as a date BP (before present) where the present is set at 1950 AD. Dates that are refined by calibration to the tree-ring sequences are described as dates cal. BP. Where possible, we have used AD and BC in this work for comparability except where we are dependent upon the carbon dates. These calibrated radio-carbon dates are identified in the text as cal. BP.

A number of traditional designations of periods of Egyptian history have emerged. For consistency, we have used the ancient chronology used by Shaw in his *Oxford History of Ancient Egypt*, which is summarised as a timeline in Table 1.1 and Figure 1.1.

TABLE 1.1 The main periods of Egyptian history referred to in this text (with commonly used abbreviations) taken from the timeline of Shaw (2000).

Palaeolithic Period	c. 700,000–5000 BC
Saharan Neolithic Period	c. 8800–4700 BC
Pre-Dynastic Period	c. 5300–3000 BC
Early Dynastic Period (ED)	c. 3000–2686 BC
Old Kingdom (OK)	2686–2160 BC
First Intermediate Period (FIP)	2160–2055 BC
Middle Kingdom (MK)	2055–1650 BC
Second Intermediate Period (SIP)	1650–1550 BC
New Kingdom (NK)	1550–1069 BC
Ramesside Period (subdivision of NK)	1295–1069 BC
Third Intermediate Period (TIP)	1069–664 BC
Late Period	664–332 BC
Ptolemaic Period	332–30 BC
Roman Period	30 BC–395 AD
Byzantine Period	395–619 AD
Persian Empire	619–639 AD
Muslim Dynastic Period	639–1517 AD
Arab and Ottoman Period	1517–1882 AD
Khedivate	1882–1953 AD
Republican Period	1953 AD–

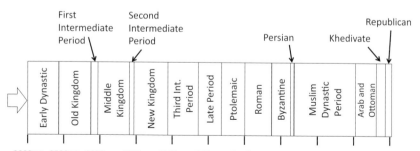

FIGURE 1.1 Ancient Egyptian timeline (after Shaw 2000)

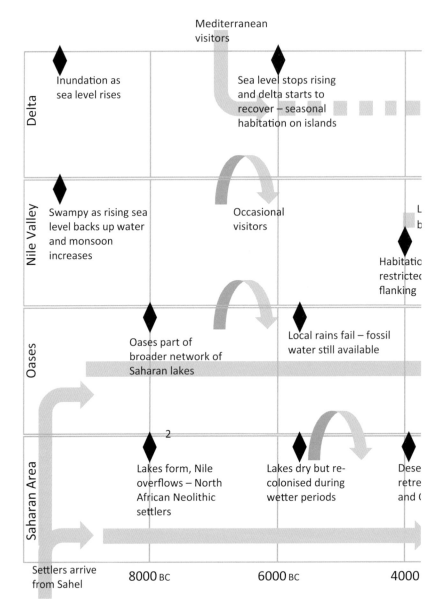

FIGURE 1.2 Diagram to show how landscapes changed with time in the main habitats of Egypt

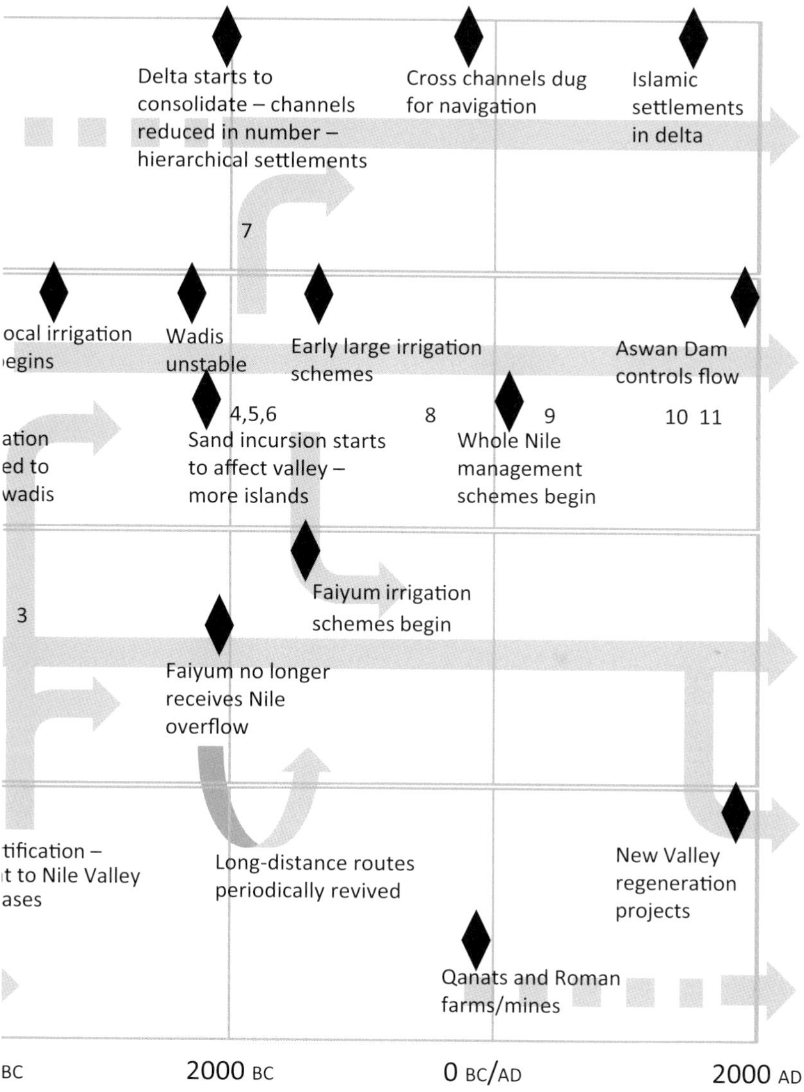

Delta starts to
consolidate – channels
reduced in number –
hierarchical settlements

Cross channels dug
for navigation

Islamic
settlements
in delta

7

ocal irrigation
·egins

Wadis
unstable

Early large irrigation
schemes

Aswan Dam
controls flow

ation
·ed to
wadis

4,5,6
Sand incursion starts
to affect valley –
more islands

8

9
Whole Nile
management
schemes begin

10 11

3

Faiyum irrigation
schemes begin

Faiyum no longer
receives Nile
overflow

tification –
t to Nile Valley
ases

Long-distance routes
periodically revived

New Valley
regeneration
projects

Qanats and Roman
farms/mines

BC   2000 BC   0 BC/AD   2000 AD

Landscape in Egypt

Broadly, Egypt can be divided into three main types of environment: the delta to the north; the Nile Valley running through the centre; and the deserts and oases that flank it. Within these environments, landscape change is relatively slow, for example the Nile migration that is perceptible over a few generations or the desertification of the Sahara that lasted around a millennium. On an even longer timescale the delta, swamped by rising sea levels, reached its marshiest around 6000 BC and spent the following 3,000–4,000 years re-consolidating its channels to form the topography we see today. Figure 1.2 shows the changes to the main habitats – the delta, the Nile Valley, the oases and the deserts. Black diamonds identify points at which changes are recorded in the archaeological record and grey arrows show how human patterns of habitation and migration have responded to the changing environment. I have also added the numbers of the chapters of this book to show how we will navigate the changes in both space and time.

Even though much of landscape change is slow, gradual change to a habitat may mean that it reaches a tipping point. For example, when the Saharan playas (seasonally drying lakes) dried up in the late Pre-Dynastic (around 4000–3600 BC), the deterioration of the food source forced many of the people living there into the Nile Valley. This influx of population also had a dramatic impact on those already resident there, as we will see. Further north in the delta, in another example, a change from very rich and diverse habitats towards a more monotonous set of channels was a driver for a more hierarchical society managed from Memphis, the node at which they met. Likewise, a period of unpredictable weather in the Nile Valley in the New Kingdom led to a series of high Nile flood levels and flash floods in the nearby desert which may have inspired the development of a landscape-wide system of channels and reservoirs in Luxor.

While it would be simplistic to present the landscape history of Egypt across these diverse environments as a linear narrative, we have tried here to highlight the main changes that occurred and their impact on the communities that lived in and migrated between them. The processes that we describe also occurred at other times at different sites in Egypt. For example, laminated windblown sand (thinly layered sand typical of that blowing into a damp environment), often associated with the First Intermediate Period, predates it in the north of Egypt at the pyramids and postdates the Middle Kingdom at Gebel al-Asr in the south. To assist the archaeologist in navigating this work, we have created a broadly chronological narrative and woven together the evidence from each of the three environments discussed. For those living in Egypt, these habitats are intimately connected.

Added to the sweeping nature of the changes is a cyclical pattern where climate warms and then cools, so the changes recorded for the Late Pleistocene, the time before the last ice age, are mimicked in a number of similar cycles occurring through the Holocene, the time since the last ice age, which we will also highlight.

2

THE GREEN DESERTS: LAKES AND PLAYAS OF THE SAHARAN WET PHASES

W E BEGIN OUR JOURNEY THROUGH SPACE AND TIME IN THE vast habitable area of the Early Holocene Sahara. Even though the uplands were still bare and inhospitable, the plains were dotted with huge ephemeral lakes and many waterholes. Some of the larger lakes contained fish and attracted game while seasonal rains supported vegetation in the damp muds of the lake beds. This was almost a 'Garden of Eden', an ideal environment through which small bands of humans roamed selecting the prime spots for habitation. The food available was so varied and abundant that, without farming or pastoralism, a largely sedentary life was possible. The Nile Valley was extremely marshy with very high floods and treacherous currents, while much of the delta, save for a few sandy islands, was under water. It follows that the most important habitat at this time was the 'desert'. Forays into the Nile Valley and delta were likely to have been risky and of short duration.

Today the Sahara is known as one of the largest wildernesses on earth, but twentieth-century travellers to the area, whether in camel caravans on the trans-Saharan trade routes or the early surveys by car, noted that there were signs of life in the desert, particularly ancient life. Caton-Thomson (1932, 1952) in her work in the Kharga Oasis discovered hand axes and flint scatters across the desert. Associated with these finds are fragments of ostrich egg-shell, occasionally shaped into beads and rock art and including subjects such as the oryx and giraffe as well as shells of aquatic snails such as *Melanoides tuberculata* (Redford and Redford 1989). Further to the south there is evidence from bones found at Kerma in Sudan (Chaix 1993) that giraffes were present there too in what is now the Bayuda Desert. Butzer (1959) described the way that Early Holocene rainfall diminished around 3500 BC and further around 3000 BC, extinguishing the populations of elephants, rhinoceroses and giraffes in the area. Only antelopes and gazelles remained to enjoy the return of rainfall during the fourth to sixth dynasties when the Gebel al-Asr area (the location of the 'Cephren diorite quarries') could be described as Khufu's snaring place (Murray 1965).

The early expeditions of the 1930s, including those of Bagnold (1935), Ball (1927, 1932, 1939) and Murray (1939), who were inspired to test the new motor cars to their limit, stumbled across remains far out in the desert, such as the stelae at Gebel al-Asr that mark the long lost 'Cephren diorite quarry' (Shaw and Bloxham, forthcoming). Since these early discoveries, many more have been made, for instance the carbon-date survey of Kuper and Kröpelin (2006). Collectively they reveal a picture of a landscape once wet that gradually dried out and was eventually overtaken by sand dunes. Evidence from mines and quarries such as Khafra's quarry at Gebel al-Asr (22°23.48'N, 31°8.3'E, Figure 2.1) shows that, even in the Old Kingdom, the climate was wetter than now, for example wells were in use at the site (Bloxham et al. 2007) and there were abundant aestivating snails (*Zootecus insularis*), which can lie dormant through the hot summers of up to seven years of drought, on the Old Kingdom surface (Shaw et al. 2001) (Figure 2.2). So, how and when did the climate change and the Saharan area become a desert?

Our current understanding of climatology suggests that these changes are part of the natural long-range climate variability experienced by the planet as global temperatures rise and fall. Of course, humans have also produced their own contributions to global warming. Although global temperature cannot be measured directly, it is possible to produce an estimate for global temperature change by considering a number of different records from different areas. Figure 2.3 shows an aggregate curve of global temperature estimated from the Greenland ice core (GISP2). The curve reveals a very abrupt upward trend in temperature at the end of the last glacial period around 12,500 years ago followed by a number of temperature oscillations.

Although Greenland may seem a far cry from the Egyptian Sahara, since what we are interested in is global climate change, it is useful as one of the best-studied and most continuous records of climate. In addition, as snow falls and becomes incorporated into the ice sheet, it remains in touch with the atmosphere for up to fifty years. The more rapidly the snow accumulates the more quickly the gas samples are isolated from atmospheric change and therefore the higher the resolution of the record. Note that the labels Old Kingdom (OK) and other periods of activity in the Khargan area all seem to be associated with periods of high global temperature. In our simplified model of global climate change these will correspond with periods of higher rainfall in the Saharan area and higher Nile floods. If replenishment of the lakes ceased and all the water evaporated, such lakes would disappear within

FIGURE 2.1 Middle Kingdom jars: part of a large group excavated at the workshop at
Quartz Ridge in the Gebel al-Asr region

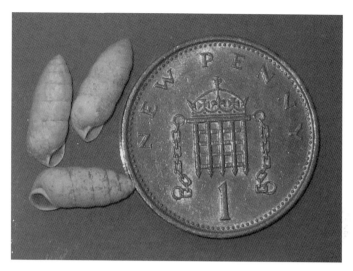

FIGURE 2.2 Aestivating snails (*Zootecus insularis*) from the Old Kingdom surface at Gebel al-Asr, with British 1 pence piece for scale

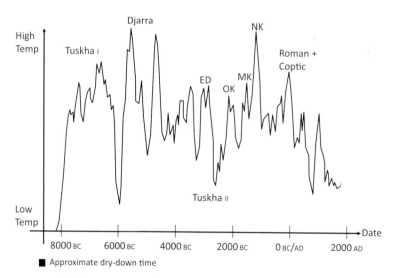

FIGURE 2.3 Global temperature change during the Holocene from Greenland Ice Sheet Project Core 2

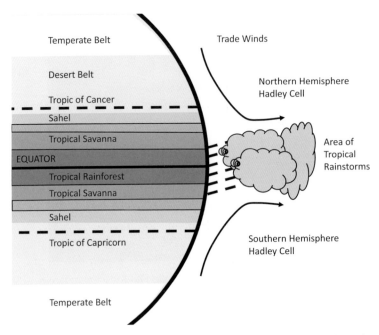

Temperate Belt

Desert Belt

Tropic of Cancer

Sahel

Tropical Savanna

EQUATOR

Tropical Rainforest

Tropical Savanna

Sahel

Tropic of Capricorn

Temperate Belt

Trade Winds

Northern Hemisphere
Hadley Cell

Area of
Tropical
Rainstorms

Southern Hemisphere
Hadley Cell

FIGURE 2.4 Diagram to show how climate changes with latitude and how the
northern and southern Hadley Cells dry the desert regions, bringing rain to the tropics

a century or less. The time taken to evaporate is shown on the diagram with
a black bar.

The main contributor to climate change over the long term – until the
eighteenth century and the industrial revolution – was fluctuation in insolation (i.e. the sun's energy that reaches earth). Fossil fuel consumption in our
post-industrial society has created another sharp rise in global temperature,
lifting it to levels that match some of the highest in the Holocene. Within
the global temperature framework, climate belts are broadly distributed by
latitude between the poles and the Equator, from the snowy ice caps to
the tropical rain forests (Figure 2.4). Warm air rising at the Equator pulls in
cooler air from higher latitudes. Since, as it warms, this cool air can absorb
more moisture, it dries out the area in its path to create deserts like the
Sahara. As it reaches the tropics, the air rises, releasing the water as tropical
rain before turning northwards at altitude and eventually sinking again to
complete the circuit. This circulation is known as the northern Hadley Cell
and is matched by a similar, mirror-image cell in the Southern Hemisphere.
Meanwhile cooling air descends at the poles, producing strong winds and
drawing high-altitude air northwards. At the surface of the planet the cold

winds are drawn southwards and eventually rise to replace the air drawn in at the poles (the Polar Cell). There is some debate on the precise structure of the air masses in the zone where the Hadley and the Polar cells collide, but it is indisputable that they and their oscillations are the source of the large amounts of weather that hit the temperate regions.

The atmospheric circulation explains how climate belts are distributed between the poles, where little sunlight falls, and the Equator, where the sun is overhead. Similar climate zones are also found in high mountains, where there may be permanent snows at the top at the same time as tropical forest at their foot. As global climate changes, the climate belts shift northwards and southwards as well as up and down any mountains.

During the ice age, when global temperatures were lowered, ice sheets stretched southwards from the North Pole into northern Europe and deposited evidence in the form of glacial sediments. Their residues are finely ground rock material known as boulder clay, which in Britain extend as far south as East Anglia, and glacial erratics (large rounded boulders dropped by glaciers) which are recorded as far south as Cornwall (e.g. the Giant's Rock). Although there were no glaciers further south, the climate also cooled there and the tropical rain belt became more tightly focussed around the Equator. Figure 2.5 shows the current distribution of vegetation (related to the climate) in North Africa and illustrates the broad-scale variation. A zigzag ornament shows the monsoon of the Ethiopian highlands and shading from dark to light shows the equatorial tropical rainforest and successively drier ecosystems towards the north through tropical savanna, sahel and desert. On the north coast of Africa, small areas of wetter Mediterranean vegetation appear as a stippled ornament.

In the Late Pleistocene and before the last glacial maximum (c. 24,500 BC), large lakes extended across North Africa among which Palaeolithic hunters roamed. Many Acheulean sites, marked mainly by flint workings, remain from these periods. However, as the ice age intensified the area became inhospitable and erosion of many of the deposits occurred. In this work, we concentrate mainly on what came after the last ice age, a period called the Holocene, the remains of which lie at the top of the sedimentary sequence and are therefore better preserved. Around 9640 BC, the last ice age ended and the large ice sheets that had covered northern Europe receded, causing the sea level to rise dramatically (Fairbanks 1989). By the same token, as the temperature rose, the belt in which tropical rains fell broadened, spreading both northwards and southwards from the Equator, turning much of Africa green and producing large lakes such as Lake Megachad (Bristow and Drake 2006) as well as supplying summer rains to the area known as the Egyptian Sahara, creating oases.

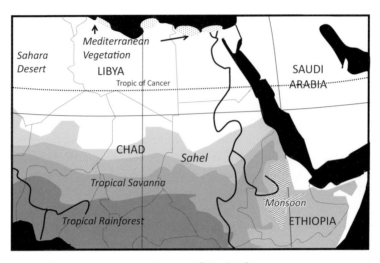

FIGURE 2.5 Contemporary vegetation map of North Africa

Global warming also re-energised the Ethiopian Monsoon, increasing the contribution of the Blue Nile to the Nile in Egypt. At times, there was so much water that the Nile overflowed into the desert (Maxwell et al. 2010), enhancing the playa lakes and oases (Figure 2.6). Caton-Thompson's work (1932) in the Kharga and Faiyum Oases retrieved many Epi-Palaeolithic technologies that seem to be associated with playa lakes and springs, such as those at Beleda near Kharga, which have subsequently dried up and disappeared. The Nile no longer overflows into Kharga except when the sluices in an artificial spillway at Toshka are opened and the flow into the Faiyum is carefully regulated at Il-Lahun. Sedimentary evidence for beaches in the two basins suggests that the Khargan lake reached a level of 170 m above sea level while the Faiyum, being further north, reached a level of c. 15 m above sea level, around 60 m above the current lake level (Koopman et al. 2016).

The shores of these basins are peppered by sparse finds of almost undatable flint débitage and discarded small grinding stones. The North Kharga Oasis Survey (Ikram and Rossi 2001 onwards) has documented many Epi-Palaeolithic tools and examples of rock art around this ancient shore, while Bagnold (1935), in his expeditions, commented that these groupings were frequently near waterholes and where rocks provided shade from the midday sun. The lakes were rich in animal and plant life brought by the water from the Nile and formed patches of habitat. Elephant and other large mammals depicted in the rock art suggest that large fauna migrated along the chains of lakes in the spillway to colonise the shores of the lake. Fish and fowl are also depicted. Even today, some populations of gazelle still gather near springs in the desert, such as the one at Ain Amur (Figure 2.7) and the last ostrich were hunted in the area in the mid-nineteenth century.

Some of the sedimentary sequences in the basins were several metres thick and, from the evidence of worm trails within the sediment (Figure 2.8), richly biodiverse. Being freshly lain, the sediments were also fertile so, where lakes dried up, plants sprang up around the basins and in the lake beds. Indeed, as the water was flowing into the remains of an earlier, much larger, Pleistocene 'Great Lake' it created an extensive area of pools and lakes separated by fertile sediment. By modelling the extent of the Holocene lakewater from the beach sediments and the modern topography available via the digital elevation model of satellite imagery, we can see that the lake in Kharga was around 3,000 km² in area and was connected through a chain of lakes to the Nile Valley. Since we know that the worms had been brought in with the water, we may conclude that other aquatic species could also have arrived and been the source of the freshwater mussels and catfish that were later eaten at the lakeside during the Neolithic (Briois et al. 2012).

However, the sedimentary evidence also reveals that at other times episodes of rain brought only a little sediment and correspondingly little water. The pools both drained into the aquifer and evaporated away, leaving parched mud encrusted with salts. During periods of drought, the plants could only persist close to sources of water, in particular places where the locally porous sandstone released the previously stored rainwater. The fossilised root systems of these plants include tree trunks around 20 cm across and roots around 10 cm in diameter, leading us to suppose that some substantial trees were able to take root and survive. As basins dried up, the plants were afflicted by drought stress and stony casts grew around their roots. These casts, known as rhizocretions (root concretions), preserve evidence of areas of grassy vegetation, shrubs and, in some areas, trees. They are often associated with ancient wells and habitations (Figure 2.9). As the levees of the Nile channel accreted, overspill became less likely so that, in Kharga, lakes that formed during the Neolithic period were entirely dependent upon local rainfall.

In the same way that the Nile overflowed into the Kharga Basin, it also overflowed into the Faiyum Depression, which also became a lake. Many prehistoric sites (Koopman et al. 2016) line the shores of this ancient and relatively persistent lake. Remains of hearths and occupation site on the beaches of the Faiyum have been carbon dated and show a peak of occupation around 5000–4000 BC. In years of low flood, the Nile did not overtop the barriers into the connections with the lakes and in the absence of rainfall

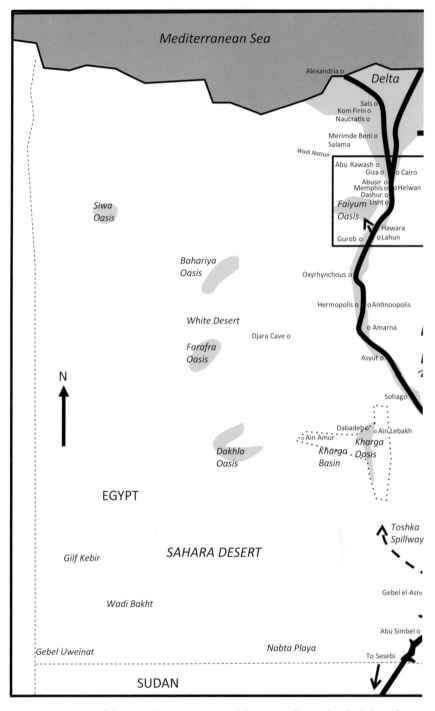

FIGURE 2.6 Map of the main Egyptian oases and the two spillways that feed them from the Nile Valley at times of very high Nile (for inset see Figure 5.6)

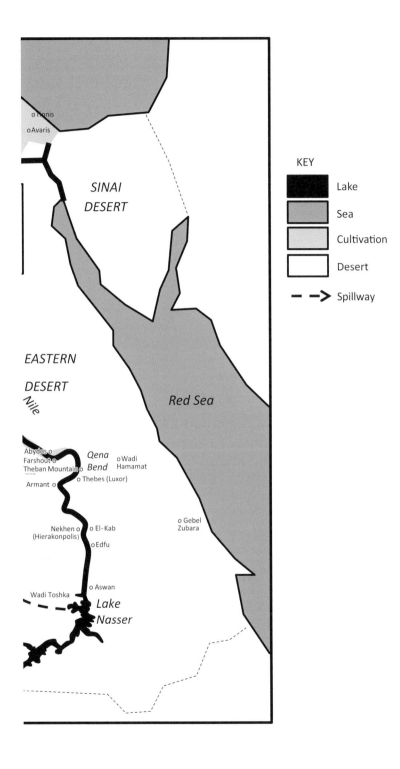

FIGURE 2.7 The temple at Ain Amur (now sadly demolished), associated with the permanent spring where gazelle still gather

FIGURE 2.8 Traces of worm feeding trails within the basin sediments at Wadi Bershama (pencil top c. 0.5 cm wide)

Traces of ancient roots

FIGURE 2.9 Traces of fossil roots (rhizocretions) in the surface water sandstone of the Nubian Sandstone Formation at Wadi Bershama, Kharga Basin (pencil c. 15 cm for scale)

this meant that the lakes dried within a few centuries. Drying conditions during the Old Kingdom meant that the Faiyum lake started to dry down quickly; it wasn't until the innovations of the Middle Kingdom that it was reactivated by human agency.

Further from the Nile, where overspill could not extend, communities still sprang up during the wetter periods. Seasonal rains fell 700 km further north into Egypt during the African Humid Period (11,000 to 5,000 years ago). These local rains recharged ground-waters and fed seasonal flows, creating lakes (Ritchie et al. 1985, Demenocal et al. 2000). Haynes (1980) suggested that the mountains and surrounding plains in south-west Egypt and north-west Sudan received from 400 to 600 mm of rainfall annually. Between the humid periods were cold, arid episodes, indicated by screes of frost-cracked chalk rubble covering the top of Early Holocene sediments. The most severe of these cold snaps were around 4.2 and 8.2 thousand years ago and resulted in the abandonment of many Saharan sites. During the arid periods NNW winds blew, drying lake beds and river floodplains to expose rich sediments before subsequently desiccating them. After the mid-Holocene, increasing desiccation rendered the erstwhile lakes saline and sterile. All that remains of these ancient lakes now are muds dissected by deep desiccation cracks and dune fields of aeolian sands.

An excellent example of life in the green Sahara, far from the River Nile, was described by Linstadter and Kröpelin (2004) at the Wadi Bakht in the Gilf Kebir. The plateau is in the far south-west of Egypt around 500 km from the Nile Valley. The earliest artefacts found in the area date from around 8000 BC and include pottery as well as lithic material, while the most recent evidence for occupation comes from around 3000 BC. A beautifully preserved section of lake sediments interspersed with sand was found in a playa basin in the wadi and shows that the ephemeral lake formed many times during the Holocene. During the Holocene, wet period summer monsoon rains fell between 8500 and 4900 BC, changing to winter rains between 4900 and 3800 BC and creating a grassy wonderland on the top of the plateau. Occupations during the early monsoon rain period seemed to be focussed on hunting and tool making, while the later occupation also involved pastoralism.

Further north from Kharga, the Djara Cave in the White Desert was on the old route between Asyut in the Nile Valley and the Farafra Oasis. This show cave has spectacular speleothems (cave deposits such as stalactites and stalagmites) but is now completely isolated. In it are examples of paintings made by hunter-gatherers in the Holocene wet phase. Analysis of a stalactite by Brook et al. (2002, 2003) suggests that these formed long ago during the Pleistocene wet phase (between 80,000 and 130,000 years ago), which also created huge lakes in the Saharan region of which only deep sediments now remain. Unfortunately, the more recent Holocene wet phase was not sufficiently wet for the stalactites to continue their growth (Brook 2003) so we have little climate context from this source.

Towards the south of Egypt, at Nabta Playa, spectacular finds were made that demonstrate the richness of life around the Saharan playa lakes (Wendorf and Schild 1998). There was sufficient groundwater, associated with ancient sand dunes buried in the mud, to sustain life, and wells from this period remain, as do many artefacts and the traces of many species of plant. The area, now completely desolate, was once rich enough for people to choose the site as a meeting place and construct megalithic remains and impressive bull tombs.

Similarly, in the Kharga Basin, Dolfin Playa to the north of Nabta Playa showed similar patterns of habitation, as did the Farafra Oasis even further north (Barich et al. 2014). All these sites suggest that rainfall was sufficiently sustained to promote vegetation over a period of around five hundred years during the Neolithic. An earlier Pleistocene large lake bed, the Great Lakes area of Haynes (1980), meant that all these areas contained rich sediment

Old Lake Bed

FIGURE 2.10 Sediment remains that reveal the locations of ancient playa lake beds in the Sahara Desert

that only required the addition of water to flourish. Rapidly changing playa lakes that formed during the rainy season could sustain plants and animals and were associated with more intense occupation than the earlier phases of lake formation. At Farafra, Barich et al. (2014) recorded that aeolian sands accumulated along slopes of hills surrounding the 'basin' of the Farafra Oasis during dry periods and were washed into it during subsequent rainy periods. The periods of occupation, determined from radiocarbon dates on hearths and ostrich eggshells, seem to correspond to times of standing water in the basin and therefore humid periods. They also identified plants that were linked to an abundance of water during a return of rains in the Early Holocene (Barich et al. 2014). These patterns mirrored those of Nabta Playa.

By studying the remains associated with these ancient lake beds (Figure 2.10), we can speculate on the animals encountered by the ancient inhabitants as well as their way of life. Finds around the playa lakes, for example Dolfin Playa in the Kharga Oasis, show how large settlements flourished around the shores as well as within the dry beds of the playas. The shoreline settlements are mostly distinguished by flint-knapping and hut rings on high ground, while activity in the lake beds includes well-digging near to sources of water

FIGURE 2.11 Large grindstones (c. 50 cm long) that are still in situ in Dolfin Playa

from the local sandstone aquifer and the grinding of grains on large (scarcely portable) grindstones. These large grindstones (Figure 2.11) were associated with the production and use of many flint tools (Figure 2.12), which suggests that the sites were abandoned as the playa flooded during the late sixth millennium BC (Karin Kindermann, personal communication).

Rock art from panels around the small lake basins shows fish, crocodiles, elephants and ostrich, among a range of as yet unidentified fowl and quadrupeds any of which might have been on the menu. The sites are also associated with images of tethered giraffes, led by men (Figure 2.13). Nearby, the abundant large grindstones, found mainly within the lake beds, also suggest that processing grain was an important part of the daily round and therefore the diet. In Kharga, scatterings of ostrich eggshell fragments around structures interpreted as wells demonstrate that eggshells were used for collecting water during the Neolithic. In many cases, these same spots were revisited by New Kingdom and Roman travellers (see Chapter 9) who added their inscriptions and broken pottery to what was already there.

Eventually the rains became erratic; in the case of Dolfin Playa, fossilised tree stumps (Figure 2.14) that were captured by a sudden influx of sediment both preserve remains from the site and demonstrate why it was abandoned.

FIGURE 2.12 Selection of tools identified as typical of the sixth millennium BC found captured by sediment at Dolfin Playa

The basin was reoccupied after the flood but, although there are abundant stone tools around the shores of the lake, it is not clear whether these were associated with the earlier or the later occupation or both.

Oval structures of limestone slabs (Figure 2.15) are found around these early lakeshores in the oases. Barich et al. (2014) excavated these at Farafra and found hearths and postholes that showed that they were the remains of shelters that probably had a superstructure of wood and animal hides. Hamdan and Lucarini (in Barich et al. 2014) also suggested that the presence of lacustrine sediments and a perennial spring located in the centre of the basin may have encouraged this area to be continuously occupied from the resumption of the humid phase of the Early Holocene, as herders were attracted to the chain of pools there. These habitations exhibited a varied economy, with hunting and sheep herding, an era described as the North African Neolithic (Garcea 2006). This occupation could be distinguished from Neolithic settlements in the Levant by the absence of crop farming. Grinding stones from the Saharan oases show that collection, grinding and consumption of grains was an important part of the diet but derived from wild species rather than domesticates.

FIGURE 2.13 Characteristic giraffe panel from Aa Rock in the Kharga Basin showing tethered giraffes led by men

FIGURE 2.14 Fossilised tree stump associated with archaeological remains dated to the period 5800–5300 BC

FIGURE 2.15 Enclosure on high ground near Fish Rock, thought to be the remains of a lakeshore dwelling similar to those found at Nabta Playa and in the Farafra Oasis

The observations from Kharga and Farafra correspond with others from across the Egyptian Sahara, from the Faiyum in the north to Nabta Playa in the south (Wendorf and Schild 1998). At Nabta Playa the longest periods of habitation are around 500 years, while stone tools typical of the Djarra B type from the White Desert further to the north (Karin Kindermann, personal communication) are typical of the period 5800 to 5300 BC. Further north again, contemporary settlements in the Faiyum focus around hearths (rather than huts) on high ground near the lake bed (Holdaway and Wendrich 2017); the remains suggest that the staple diet was fish enhanced by grains, occasional game hunting and limited pastoralism. Well-preserved baskets sunk into the ground show that grain was already being stored at this period. Phillips et al. (2012) showed that the grains depended on the winter rains for their cultivation. Unfortunately, the Faiyum shore dwellers were eventually forced to move away from the lake and cut clearings in the surrounding forest to prevent hippopotamus depredation of their food supply (Shirai 2016).

Closer to the Nile Valley and the delta, Neolithic sites also sprang up, like the one at Merimde, where houses were dispersed along the flanks of a wadi adjacent to a pool. Merimde is a Neolithic site on the outskirts of the Western Nile Delta, which has over the last century become a source of intense interest and focus for geo-archaeologists keen to explore the adaptation of human civilisation to its external environment. It is the earliest known settlement in the delta area and therefore provides crucial data about the first human communities to inhabit it, especially as evidence of an evolving civilisation spanning perhaps 600 years has been identified. The first excavations occurred between 1929 and 1939, when Hermann Junker and other scholars attempted to chronologically sequence events at the site through the detailed examination of archaeology found in the strata. Pottery, flints, tools and skeletons were collected, and the finds were used as evidence to map out the pattern of human habitation during Pre-Dynastic times. Unfortunately, the work was never properly published, as the documents were lost in the Second World War.

Initial explorations identified two Pre-Dynastic deltaic civilisations – the Merimde Abu Ghalib, which covered several hills where hordes of very small flint tools were found, and Merimde Beni Salama, found midway between Cairo and Kom Hamada. Continuing studies of Merimde (Butzer 1976) have explored the adaption of man to a landscape battered by extreme environmental and topographic conditions and in a state of constant climatic flux. The most recent and extensive studies indicate that the area was inhabited during the Late Pleistocene, on a site far larger than originally expected, and with far wider agricultural use of the landscape (Rowland and Tassie 2014). Plotting finds from excavations of the site and known climate patterns shows human habitation closely following the line of high water level in the Nile channels. During low rainfalls levels, for example during the last glaciations, gezirehs (sandy islands) and channels were exposed and became the focus for the civilisations that made their homes there. In times of high rainfall, for example the Early Holocene, populations could spread out along the hinterlands of the Nile, now lush with vegetation and capable of supporting larger numbers of people.

Merimde provides a captivating picture of a Neolithic community adapting over time. The earliest settlements were characterised by polished and unpolished pottery, decorated with a herringbone design. Later settlements were capable of constructing complex wooden structures, suggesting an organised societal structure. Tools evolved using a mix of materials to enhance their performance, for example flint tools with wooden, bone or ivory handles, demonstrating a more sophisticated approach to craftsmanship than evinced earlier. Examination of the remains of houses also exposes a relatively complex organisational structure, with silos, storage pits and granaries dotted

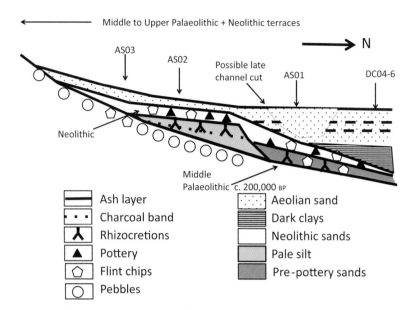

FIGURE 2.16 Section through the Neolithic terrace at Wadi Gamal, Merimde Beni Salama; DC04-6, AS01, AS02 and AS03 are the locations of drill (DC) and auger cores (AS)

around the site. These may provide evidence of some form of collective or higher society and introduce the idea of individual ownership.

The style of the pieces of pottery is congruent with the Nubian pottery of the time; this fact and the existence of other non-indigenous materials means that there may have existed some form of trade or at least a connection with other tribes or foreign lands (perhaps Bedouin from the Sahara or North Africans). In fact, despite the early development of pottery-making in the Western Desert, it was not until the Merimde Neolithic that clay figurines became common (Eiwanger 1992).

Augering of the sediments at Merimde Beni Salama (Figure 2.16) shows how Middle Palaeolithic activity at the site predated a silt terrace produced during a period of very high sea level. A charcoal-rich band within the silt shows that human activity in the area continued during the terrace formation. The map in Figure 2.17 shows how later Neolithic dwellings were situated on the vegetated surface of the silt terrace, adjacent to a body of stagnant water around 4 m deep that left a bed of clay-rich sediment. I have labelled this lake 'Hippo Pool' in deference to the hippopotamus tibia bones that were used in the semi-sunken huts as doorsteps. Flint quarries further up the wadi were also in use at this period. The stagnant water of the pool was later filled with aeolian sand from which the ferruginous coating

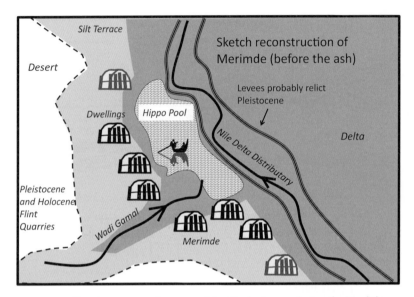

FIGURE 2.17 Sketch reconstruction map of the Merimde area during the Neolithic habitation showing the probable extent of the still-water pool (Hippo Pool) and the way in which the Neolithic huts were located on the terraces that flank the Wadi Gamal adjacent to the pool and below the flint quarries

(desert varnish) dissolved in the anoxic water. Two ash bands for which Merimde is known are found within the sand and, if these are associated with the eruption of Thera (yet to be tested), would place the infilling in a period that included the New Kingdom, a comparable period to that of sand movements around Dashur. A later rainwater channel, flowing down the Wadi Gamal, recut these sandy sediments.

At the end of the Saharan Neolithic the lakes and playas started to dry up and infill, but there were still some places with access to fresh groundwater, the Nile Valley and the oases. All of the Kharga, Dakhla, Farafra, Bahariya and Siwa system of oases provided refugia (places to which people retreated) from the effects of desertification. In Kharga, local groundwater persisted into the New Kingdom and Roman Period around wells and qanats into the Nubian Aquifer (see Dabadeb in Chapter 9). Artesian water, pushed to the surface along a major fault, is still available near to the town of Kharga today.

The evidence for climate change is subtle but abundant and takes many forms, revealing that, even since the end of the Saharan Neolithic, there have been episodes of milder and wetter climate. Although evidence for climate change appears in sediments it may also be deduced from other sources. Architects have noted that some Old Kingdom buildings were furnished

Millet seed grains

Millet seed grains
in Roman plaster

FIGURE 2.18 Sample of plaster from the Church at 'Ain Lebakh in the Kharga Basin

with gutters and rainwater spouts, although by the New Kingdom these features were abandoned, presumably because they had become redundant. In another line of evidence, New Kingdom houses at Amarna (Spence 2004) had a main chamber which was ventilated by a north-facing wind hood, a structure on the roof that funnelled the trade wind through the main living quarters, demonstrating that trade winds were established by this time. By combining all the available sources of evidence, we create a clearer picture of landscape change and the human response to it.

Indeed, even humble building materials change in response to climate, since the local sands and muds that are available are the product of the environment in which they have accumulated. For example, the Roman church at 'Ain Lebakh in the Kharga Depression contains desert-rounded sand grains as keying in the plaster layers (Figure 2.18). The sand in the plaster is composed of very well-rounded and yellowed quartz grains that are typical of the grains produced by wind erosion in a desert. These grains, known to geologists as 'millet seed grains', appear in the natural desert surface. In Roman Oasis pottery, the fabrics are rich in rounded grains although these are absent in the Neolithic fabrics from the area (from sherds in the British Museum Wendorf Collection and the North Kharga Oasis Survey studies and Leslie Warden, personal communication). In northern Sudan, the same rhizocretions, rich in gypsum, already created by plants in stress were reused to make plaster in New Kingdom Kush (Van Pelt 2013).

The oases are the main survivals from the earlier 'Green Sahara', although some mountains such as the Gilf Kebir, Gebel Uweinat and the plateau at 'Ain Amur in the Kharga Depression attracted sufficient direct rainfall to sustain a population long after the rest of the Sahara had been deserted. In the early twentieth century, Bagnold (1935) in his travels through the Sahara encountered a group still living tenuously on the spring water at Gebel Uweinat (though he reported that even that group had gone by the time he returned a few years later). During the last ice age, trade winds like those that blow today were prevalent. However, Drake and Bristow (2006) show that as the climate warmed at the end of the ice age and the area of monsoon winds came northwards there was a change to seasonal south-westerly summer winds. By 4000 BP the monsoon had failed again.

The desiccation of the Sahara and the establishment of trade winds bringing sand and creating dune fields were accompanied by deflation – erosion of the soils and sediments by wind and sand action. This deflation is relatively rapid; there are records of over a metre of deflation since Roman times in parts of the Kharga Oasis. Roman farmers commonly used the power of erosion to remove salt that had accumulated in the fields, leaving them fallow while the salt was eroded before replanting them. The amount of erosion is visible in Figure 2.19; it shows how the soil, itself part of a former lake bed visible to the left of the wall, was dug and stone-lined to form a well. Some rhizocretions preserved in the soil show that shrubs bene-fited from the local water supply too. However, since that time, not only has the well dried but over a metre of the surrounding sediment has been removed by wind erosion, leaving little but the wall and a few rhizocretions remaining. As the soils and sediments are deflated, the artefacts that were on or in them are exposed and left lying upon the surface, often in a surreal juxtaposition of materials and periods. With this type of residue, little can be done to reconstruct the original stratigraphy.

We are currently in a dry phase of Saharan history but with modern climate warming the phase is already ending, with small playa lakes reforming in recent years. The lake in Figure 2.20 originally formed in the winter of 2013 and, at its peak, contained several metres of water. Salt crusts around the shores of the lake showed that it was evaporating during the day but that at night the lake level still continued to sink as water drained into the local sandstones. Several species of plant germinated around shores of the lake; however, with evaporation and the concentration of naturally occurring salts

FIGURE 2.19 Erosion of Roman wall from a well in Wadi Bershama near Kharga

Lake Ephemera January 2014

FIGURE 2.20 Dried up lake bed in the Sahara Desert shown one year after rain

in the lake water, the centre of the lake was brackish by the time it finally
dried up. Little dents in the lake bed, produced subsequently by a brief
shower of rain, showed that there had been a little refreshment of the basin,
but in general the plants survived through being tolerant of aridity and by
tapping the stored groundwater. A year later, the lake still provided a habitat
for birds and visiting gazelle. We hope that current archaeological exploration can record the delicate ancient remains before they are overwritten by
the settlers of this next green phase.

In summary, during the Early Holocene there was little habitable land
beyond the Saharan lakes. The Nile Valley was swamped as river water
backed up against the rising sea levels in the Mediterranean and became
marshy. During the annual summer inundation, the Nile, now augmented
by an increased Ethiopian Monsoon, rose in the Nile canyon and in places
overflowed into the wadi mouths and sometimes overspilled to augment large
lakes in the desert such as the Faiyum. To the north conditions in the delta
were also swampy, although low islands of sand left behind from the higher
sea levels of the Pleistocene emerged from the many interconnected marsh-
land channels. These islands may have been accessible at times of low Nile
but were only suitable for temporary habitation. The shores of the wet areas
were nonetheless suitable for exploitation, although the inhabitants probably
chose to live a little further away in the wadi mouths and flanking hills.

3

THE CLIMATE SEESAW: THE BALANCE BETWEEN HUNTER-GATHERING AND FARMING IN THE WADIS AND MARSHES OF THE NILE VALLEY

T HE NILE VALLEY AND DELTA HAD BEEN RATHER INHOSPITABLE during the wet phases of the Early Holocene. Towards the end of the Saharan Neolithic, both flood levels and local rainfall were reduced, rendering the Nile tamer. At the same time the reduction in local rainfall in the Saharan region drove people out of the deserts, making the Nile a popular destination. Flanking the Nile, the wadis were well vegetated and provided ready access to the desert, as did the terraces that flanked the marshes of the delta. A combination of hunting in the wadis with fishing and gathering in the Nile Valley was augmented by some herding of sheep, goats and cattle. When seasonal rains refreshed the Sahara, the wadis also provided easy access to the playas. The Nile, now the lifeblood of Egypt, began its rise to supreme importance.

The Nile and its expanse of catchment have been globally significant to the civilisations and cultures of the region for millennia, providing an important corridor for the movement of people and animals throughout the Holocene. Flowing for 2,700 km from the south of the Equator to the shores of the Mediterranean and covering an area of 3 million square kilometres, it is unique both in size and variety of river basin. The main contributors to the Nile in Egypt are the White Nile, which rises in equatorial Africa, and the Blue Nile, which rises in the highlands of Ethiopia; these join at Khartoum in Sudan. The Nile is unusual in that it has few other perennial tributaries, so its character is remarkably similar for much of its course northwards from Khartoum. The catchment supports a vast range of ecosystems and has played a central role in the development of a rich diversity of communities.

The Nile floodplain in Egypt currently forms a green cultivated strip that cuts north–south across the Sahara Desert. To many, the river appears immutable but the current form is the result of a tempestuous past. The river today is the result of many phases of development (Said 1981) but for our purposes it is sufficient to begin six million years ago with the erosion of what is described as the Nile Canyon, the valley bounded by cliffs through which the Nile flows. The early Nile (Eonile) flowed approximately along its current course towards the Mediterranean Sea but, at that time, tectonic collision between Europe and Africa had shut the Straits of Gibraltar. With no new water flowing from the Atlantic into the Mediterranean, seawater evaporated and it shrank. Some rivers still supplied the Mediterranean Basin but as the sea level lowered the water became extremely salty, somewhat like a giant version of the Dead Sea today. Also as the sea level lowered the Eonile eroded away its sediment in an attempt to cut down to sea level, creating a deep canyon, similar in scale to the Grand Canyon, which stretched as far south as Aswan. Local tributaries in Egypt also cut down to try to keep level with the Eonile, creating deep valleys, now known as the Radar Valleys since they are detectable on radar images of the desert. The meandering of the modern Nile is constrained by this canyon to a narrow strip no more than 12 km wide.

In time, by around three to four million years ago, the tectonic pressure around the Straits of Gibraltar was released and water poured through the gap into the Mediterranean Basin and from there through the Bosphorus to the Black Sea, re-flooding the entire area and inundating the Nile Delta. The precursor of the Nile, by this time known as the Palaeonile, continued to flow and, augmented by sediment derived locally from Egypt, gradually filled up the Nile Canyon with gravel and sandy sediments; these can still be reached around 20 m below the surface of the Nile muds. The side valleys, which today form the many wadis of Egypt, also refilled with sediment and, during the Pleistocene, when the sea level was a little higher than today, the sediments accumulated to a level around 2 m above the irrigated land of northern Egypt. During the last ice age, the sea level fell once again and the sands and gravels deposited by the Palaeonile were again dissected. The raised sandbanks, left behind as the Nile eroded down again, are known locally as gezirehs (Arab. 'island').

At the end of the last ice age, the sea level rose once again, inundating the areas between the gezirehs, which, forming an archipelago, became a popular site for mid-Holocene habitation. The annual inundation ensured that fresh, fertile sediment was deposited year by year onto the lower ground of the floodplain. With time, farmers anticipated and managed the Nile and its flood so that agriculture burgeoned. In the late nineteenth century, Muhammad Ali had a dam constructed at Aswan to manage the flood and increase agricultural productivity. However, in the late 1960s a new Aswan High Dam was created that could completely control the flood. A large area was flooded as water filled the new reservoir to form Lake Nasser, a lake that is around 350 km long. The construction of the dam required the relocation of numerous people and the relocation of monuments, including the Temple of Abu Simbel.

In the annual flood cycle, the White Nile maintains a steady flow, but the Blue Nile, with its highly seasonal swelling of waters from the Ethiopian Monsoon, causes an annual inundation (for more details see Woodward et al. 2007). Small wonder that life in the Nile Valley started to revolve around the flood and the seasons were determined by it. First came Akhet (June to September) when the floodwaters rose and no farming could take place, although mass transport of goods could occur since the water was deeper and more extensive than at other times of the year. As the flood receded it ushered in the season of Peret (October to February) when as much of the land as possible was used for agriculture. Activities included sowing and reaping crops in the irrigated flood basins as well as grazing of stock or even hunting in the thickets and marshes that fringed the valley. By March the harvest was ready and Shemu (March to May) began. Once the crops were in, preparation for the next flood season began: clearing ditches and repairing embankments ready for the flood to return.

Although we can no longer observe the annual flood of the Nile, fortunately we still have historic maps and traveller accounts as well as the exceptional photographic record of Rudolf Lehnert and Ernst Landrock, who ran a photographic business in Cairo during the early twentieth century and who photographed the Nile from all angles and in all seasons. For example, in their image of Dashur, the settlement, huddled on a piece of high ground, appears to be a ship afloat in the floodwaters of the Nile Valley, while a photograph of the pyramids at Giza taken at a similar time of year shows boats approaching the monuments. Although the inundation became a regular feature of life on the Nile, climatic change meant that there were times of high and low flood. Macklin and his co-workers (Macklin et al. 2015) suggest that these recent effects of climate change on the Nile can be divided into five significant stages, characterised by major changes and shifts in lake levels and river flows (Table 3.1). Even though the seasonality of the Nile floods did not change during the Holocene, the magnitude of flood events changed considerably and progressively as climate changed (Macklin et al. 2015). Sudden reductions in river flow caused widespread channel and floodplain contraction, and these events recurred frequently over the course of six to seven thousand years, affecting riverine societies dramatically.

TABLE 3.1 Stages in the development of the Nile

Stage	Date	
1	6400–5800 cal. BC	Significant hydrological variability, characterised by high to low water levels in key lakes contracting channels and floodplain due to drier conditions and reduced flow.
2	4500 cal. BC	Next major shift in Nile catchment, falling temperatures in Kilimanjaro and low water levels in Lake Victoria and Tana, coinciding with diminishing river flows in the Nile Delta.
3	2800–2450 cal. BC	Falling water levels, decreasing flow and cooler temperatures.
4	After 450 cal. BC	Water levels never exceed those recorded before 500 cal. BC.
5	1450–1650 cal. AD	Falling and low lake levels in the Blue Nile and decreasing flows in the Nile Delta.

During periods of low global temperature, the Ethiopian Monsoon is reduced and, during the last ice glacial maximum, even switched off so that the Nile is fed only by the White Nile. Conversely, with global temperatures higher, as they are now, the Ethiopian Monsoon, with its consequent inundation, is restored. Local rainfall that falls in Egypt during times of higher global temperature augments the Nile rushing in to it from the wadis (Rodrigues et al. 2000, Stanley et al. 2003). In Ethiopia, the monsoon erodes the basalts of the highlands, adding dark red mud to the Nile which turns the river red as it travels down to Egypt, arriving between June and October. As the river channel becomes very full it eventually spills over the river's natural levees and spreads across the floodplain. At times of very intense inundation, Nile water broadens into the mouths of neighbouring wadis, extending the cultivable area of the Nile floodplain.

The changing impact of the river on the cultures and beliefs of the peoples of the region can be seen in the literature and art of the the last five thousand years, from and great irrigation-based civilisations of the ancient Egyptians, with their strong association and dependence on the river, to the modern-day Egyptians who strive to manage, harvest and control the Nile's vast power through dam construction (Woodward et al. 2007). Stanley and Warne (1994) posit that it was the maturation of deltas near sea level that gave rise to civilisations across the globe as sea levels stabilised in the mid-Holocene after a period of rapid rise (Pennington 2016). Together with these successful and long-living civilisations came developments in agricultural practices and the emergence of more complex social organisation, arguably as a response to the climatic changes they were experiencing at the time. Studies of areas close to the Nile, such as Faiyum, demonstrate similar patterns, with periods of occupation and abandonment throughout the Holocene.

Human Adaption in Response to Climate Change

Farming and herding in the Nile Valley began around the late sixth millennium BC. Macklin et al. (2015) explore the correlation of adoption of new farming practices and the development and success of new civilisations with changes in climate, in particular channel and floodplain contraction. Macklin speculates that a period of river channel contraction would be advantageous to farmers by exposing nutrient-rich sediment on the floodplain and making the exposed areas less hazardous and more manageable for agriculture. An analogous way of life persists among the Bedouin of the Eastern Desert of Egypt today. Joseph Hobbs (1990) describes a way of life in which Bedouin used local knowledge to navigate the desert, anticipating where rain had fallen and where water could be found at different times of the year. Through a mixture of harvesting resources and pasturing their flocks where fodder could be found, the Bedouin are able to subsist in the wilderness (Murray 1935). At times, anticipating future rains, they plant seeds in a basin and, without tilling the crop, they hope to return at a later date to find a harvest, a sort of minimalist agriculture.

The development of farming and riverine societies in the Nile Valley in the late sixth millennium BC occurred far later than in south-west Asia (Kuper and Kröpelin 2006). The transition to the Neolithic economy occurred after a major period of channel and floodplain contraction between 6150 and 5750 cal. BC, coinciding with drier conditions. This was advantageous as nutrients and rich sediments were spread across former floodplains. The channels consequently became less hazardous, more exposed and more manageable for farmers. In Kerma in Upper Nubia (Welsby 2001), there was a shift of occupation after 5300 BC to alluvial plains which had been previously unoccupied. This shift was associated with the aridification of the local environment, although Nile records indicate Neolithic settlements of the valley floor coincided with higher river flows than prior to 7500 cal. BC.

Unfortunately, within the Nile Valley and Delta, evidence for early farming in the diverse habitats of the maturing river system are scarce or non-existent due to the rapid sedimentation in this area that buries the evidence before 2000 BC (Pennington et al. 2016, Yann Tristant, unpublished book). However, areas where there is large movement of mineral material are those that have the most fertile soils. For example, Vesuvius, an active volcano on the Italian peninsula, although cataclysmically dangerous, provides very fertile soils which have supported vibrant human populations; similarly the actively faulting basins of western Turkey present the perfect growing environment for fruit and other foodstuffs. We expect that the diverse habitats of the Nile Valley were ideal for fishing and fowling, supported by harvesting of wild grains.

As the immature river system gave way to a more mature river system with lower environmental diversity and more stable channels, this habitat became less fertile and required the adoption of agricultural practices and techniques in the delta that also spread to the floodplains (Pennington et al. 2016). Hence, changing diets were a notable feature of this transition. Earlier reliance was on aquatic resources, and fish, in particular, were enormously important, with remains of burnt fish prevalent, for example, at Sais in the Nile Delta. There are also prolific offerings of fish at temples during this time in contrast to a relative absence of mammals or any complex or highly developed animal husbandry techniques. After the stabilisation of the channels this appears to no longer be the case (Pennington et al. 2016 and see Chapter 7).

Some scholars, for example Kupar and Kröpelin (2006), identify the seesawing of climate between warm, humid conditions and cooler, arid conditions as the motor of evolution in North Africa. As people begin to control the cycle of grasses and other plants, they select and sow varieties that meet their requirements. Thus, the involvement of farmers causes the adaptation of wild grasses, for example wheat, that have a higher yield even if this means that they are more intensive to farm. Ethnobotanists who study botanical remains from archaeological sites, including the burnt grains in remains from hearths, see a change in the plants as domestication proceeds. Egypt's neighbours to the north-east in Mesopotamia had already developed domesticated species which could conveniently be imported to the Egyptian Delta. Phillips (2012) suggests that people adopted the domestic grains when environmentally viable and sensible to do so, meaning that the changing environmental conditions triggered drastic changes in agricultural adoption.

As the deserts dried, Saharan communities continued to flourish but were concentrated into the residual wet areas. These were terraces of sediment fringing the river floodplain, the flanking wadis and the oases. The remaining grasslands of the hinterland still provided ample food when combined with a diet rich in fish, sourced from the Nile. By the Early Dynastic Period, unification swept across Egypt, forging both north and south into one political entity under the leadership of Hierakonpolis, a large site on the Saharan bank of the Nile near Edfu. This innovation may reflect the concentration of people and resources into the Nile Valley from the encroaching desert (Kuper and Kröpelin 2006). At this time, the wadis were still eminently habitable

FIGURE 3.1 Vegetation in modern Peruvian wadis showing how we imagine the wadis around Hierakonpolis during the heyday of the site (photo Nicholas Warner)

(see Figure 3.1) and, thanks to the protective vegetation that reduced the impact of rainfall, there was little run off or sand erosion.

As the Nile became the focus of habitation, new important sites such as Abydos were founded where the pastoral ranges of the desert met the now tamer Nile (Dufton 2008). From a human perspective, the loss of the desert ranges was a humanitarian disaster, as the displaced poured into the Nile Valley, but it led to a host of cultural interactions that are often argued to have resulted in the formation of the first unified Egyptian state (Hassan 1996); it may also explain the large numbers of novel artefact forms encountered at Hierakonpolis (Adams 1995, Friedman 2009), which is particularly well known for its pink, flaked flint ceremonial knives and schist palettes (Quibell 1900). The significance of Hierakonpolis may be that it was an arrival point in the Nile Valley for those fleeing the Great Lakes area via the Kharga Oasis (see Figure 2.6).

Dufton (2008) considered how Hierakonpolis and other contemporary sites were set in the landscape. He reconstructed the vegetated wadi ranges and how they connected the Saharan grasslands to the rather swampy Nile Valley (Figure 3.2). Habitation was generally in the wadi mouths and on the fringing terraces of the valley. Climate change during the Early Dynastic period led to diminution of the wadi vegetation, with wadi collapse followed

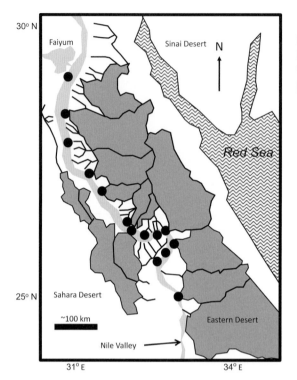

David Dufton Tasian/
Badarian Sites and the
Wadi Ranges of the
Egyptian Deserts

FIGURE 3.2 Pre-Dynastic wadi catchments reconstructed by Dufton (2008)

by sand influx from the now arid Saharan region. River catchment basins derived from the topography of the Sahara Desert are annotated with dark dots to show the locations of Badarian-aged settlements where the large ranges connected with the Nile Valley.

Dufton also reconstructed the migrations of the Nile in the Abydos area (Figure 3.3). He concluded that although the Nile was probably close at hand during the formation of the site in the Early Dynastic, it soon migrated away (see Chapter 4 for more details of river migration). The important connectivity with the desert remained, however, and, when conditions in the desert seem to have become wetter in the New Kingdom, a programme of refurbishment was conducted, using a canal to bring materials to the site. Important sites like Abydos continued to be connected by cross-desert routes where these were practicable but they were probably the province of military patrols and specialist traders and travellers.

Usai (2005) suggests that the settlement shift from the desert to the Nile may not have been cataclysmic, although it was the touchstone for political

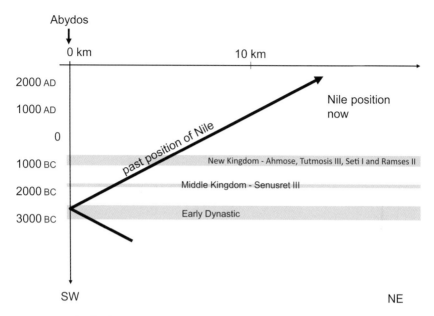

FIGURE 3.3 Dufton's (2008) reconstruction of the way that the Nile has migrated around Abydos; the x-axis shows the distance across the floodplain from Abydos while the y-axis shows time

unification along the Nile Valley. Her work in the Second Cataract region of the Neolithic shows that there was some degree of transhumance between Nile and desert habitats during the course of the year. The failure of rains and desiccation of playa lakes may simply have led to fewer and shorter journeys made into the deserts. Conversely, during periods of amelioration, folk memory as well as direct observation probably prompted more and extended visits to revived habitats away from the Nile. Today, evidence for ancient vegetation in the wadis remains in the stony lumps known as rhizocretions that litter the muddy terraces that flank the Nile Valley. Rhizocretions form around the roots of plants that live under drought stress and can be seen forming around plants in northern Sudan today. Although the plants that formed the rhizocretions at Hierakonpolis are long dead, the rhizocretions themselves are evidence that they once flourished there (Figure 3.4).

Hierakonpolis is an excellent example of a site at the transition from life adjacent to the Nile to life in the Nile Valley. There is evidence for continuous habitation there from the Pre-Dynastic to the New Kingdom, but it is for the exceptional Pre-Dynastic finds that Nekhen (later known as Hierakonpolis) is best known. The site is dominated by a very large

FIGURE 3.4 Large rhizocretions from the terraces of the Arkin Formation at Hierakonpolis, which lead us to think that when the settlement was located here the terrace was abundantly vegetated with large shrubs (pencil c. 15 cm long)

mud-brick enclosure, known as the Khasekhemwy Enclosure. Early excavations by Quibell and Green (Quibell 1900) in the late nineteenth century revealed many rare items including ripple-flaked, flint knives that had been turned pink by heat treatment. They were too large to have been of more than ceremonial use and were accompanied by a ceremonial mace head and schist palette attributed to Narmer, one of the early kings of Egypt. The early excavations have been followed by many other investigations (Hoffman et al. 1986, Adams 1995), which have revealed wooden buildings, elephant and baboon burials and many other discoveries. Abundant rhizocretions at the site (see Figure 3.4) reveal that the silt terraces that flank the Nile were well vegetated in the past, sustained by local rainfall during the mid-Holocene (Hoffman et al. 1986) and therefore relatively stable.

Augering in the area around the temple and the wadi mouth (Figure 3.5) revealed that during the late Pre-Dynastic the island flank became subject to incursions of desert clay during wadi-wash events that intensified during the Early Dynastic. The auger core log also reveals that an early but mixed unit

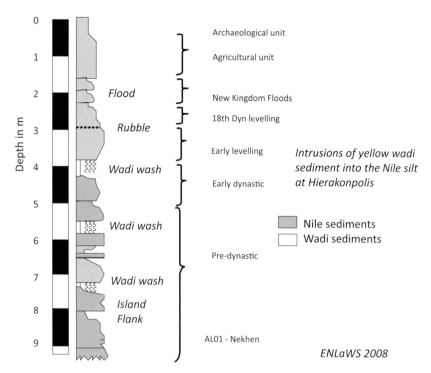

FIGURE 3.5 Example sediment log from augering (AS01) from Nekhen (later known as Hierakonpolis) near to the Old Kingdom Temple

followed these events (at 3–4 m depth) and seems to represent levelling in preparation for construction of the Old Kingdom temple. A similar but later event was probably the result of the New Kingdom refurbishment of the site. With time the floodplain built up around the abandoned site and the area was subject to flooding during the later New Kingdom before returning to the floodplain and agriculture. It continued to be farmed until the initiation of archaeological activity at the site in the late nineteenth century. From a series of auger cores such as this, a landscape reconstruction can be proposed showing how the environment of Hierakonpolis has changed over the past six thousand years (Figure 3.6).

By considering the results from Hierakonpolis in the context of similar cores in the Edfu and Hagr Edfu area we can propose an extended pattern of landscape-scale changes for the Edfu floodplain (Figure 3.7). The river is first attested during the Naqqada I Period at the south side of the valley and adjacent to the silt terraces at Hierakonpolis. It had presumably arrived at this point by migration from the northern side. With time (shown moving up

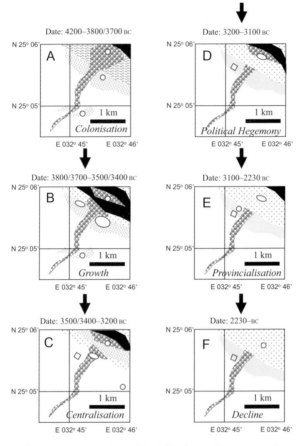

FIGURE 3.6 Landscape reconstruction of the Hierakonpolis area over the past 6,000 years (after Adams 1995)

the page), the river began to migrate back towards the north, turning during the Middle Kingdom and arriving to the north of the Nekhen mound (but not crossing it) during the New Kingdom. Further sweeps across the valley can be inferred from historic maps. This sweeping motion of Nile channels became a theme of life in the valley and is discussed further in Chapter 4.

So, by the Pre-Dynastic the wadis were perceived as the ideal site for habitation but they did not remain so for long. As the site of Hierakonpolis also reveals, at the same time as the Nile channels were stabilising, the wadis that flanked the Nile were also changing since the reduction in rainfall destabilised the wadi sands and gravels (Figure 3.8). Although, when rainfall is plentiful, vegetation stabilises the wadi floor and absorbs rainfall, preventing erosion of the sediments, as rainfall drops and vegetation becomes sparse,

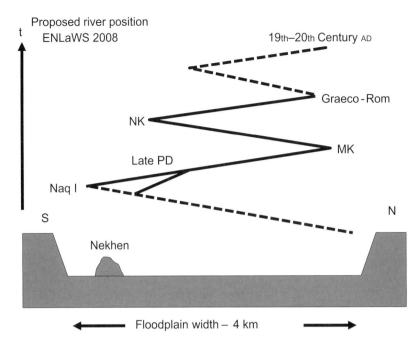

FIGURE 3.7 Proposed pattern of river movements for the Edfu floodplain since the Pre-Dynastic

the wadis flow. The evidence for wooden architecture (www.hierakonpolis-online.org) at Hierakonpolis suggests that the denudation was assisted by humans who felled trees, culled firewood for brewing and baking (Adams 1995) and grazed animals over shrubs and grasses, leading to wadi washout. At Hierakonpolis, boreholes show evidence for three successive collapses, each more dramatic than the previous one. As conditions became more arid, the rate of erosion dropped (Goudie and Wilkinson 1977). Eventually, although all the vegetation died, there was no longer any rainfall to erode the sediment and the wadi became relatively stable again.

A similar pattern of erosion is seen elsewhere in Egypt. In the north at Giza (Lehner et al. 2009) a water tank in the wadi through Khentkawes town was eroded as water rushed down the wadi and later repaired. Work by Senussi and Jones (1997) in the Cairo area also shows a similar pattern of wadi washouts that produced tongues of sandy sediment that intruded the muds of the Nile Valley (Figure 3.9). They reveal that the early settlements were in the wadis that flanked the Nile Valley. With time, these settlements were destroyed or abandoned as the wadis became unstable and settlement moved instead to the banks of the Nile. Elsewhere, remains of Badarian and other Early Dynastic settlements survive in the wadi mouths where

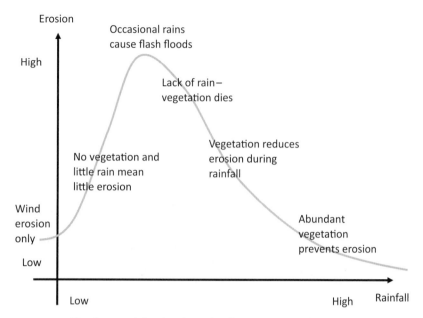

FIGURE 3.8 Sketch curve (after Goudie and Wilkinson 1977) to show how increasing rainfall affects erosion rates in an arid environment

the desert catchments disgorge into the Nile Valley (Dufton and Branton 2009). What is clear is that occupants of the area even then, some thousand years prior to the supposed dramatic climate chaos of the First Intermediate Period, were adapting to changing landscape and climate.

With life in the Nile Valley stabilising and the deserts increasingly hostile, forays to the known sources of raw materials, particularly precious stone, became hazardous and labour-intensive. It required a powerful king like Khafra to send missions into the desert, for example to Gebel el-Asr, an area known for the 'Cephren diorite quarries', far in the south of Egypt. This area, close to the border with Sudan, was around 800 km from the great pyramid of Khafra at Giza, where he used the stone hewn from the quarries (Figure 3.10). The Old Kingdom quarries at the site indicate the extent to which the climate and landscape have changed.

During the Old Kingdom both Khufu and Khafra sent expeditions to the south of Egypt to the quarries of Gebel el-Asr to procure stone for their pyramid projects at Giza. At the quarries, ramps and trackways were cut into the lake bed sediments so that very large blocks of stone could be loaded onto sledges for transport to the Nile Valley (Shaw et al. 2001) (Figure 3.10). We know from a copper chisel, now in the Egyptian Museum in Cairo, that

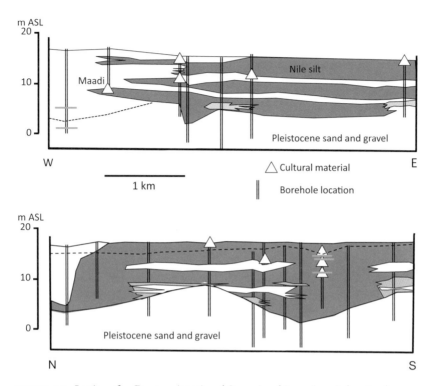

FIGURE 3.9 Section after Branton (2008) and Senussi and Jones (1997) showing how tongues of sand intrude the silts of the Nile Valley in the Giza area as wadis are denuded of vegetation and sediment collapses

the quarrymen were organised into the watches of a boat. Indeed, texts also suggest that the quarry missions were manned partly by soldiers, who travelled along the Nile in boats, and partly by slaves or other captives who were compelled to work with them. Accounts also suggest that quarry work was not a popular deployment and that the cost in lives of men and beasts was part of the value of the rare materials won from the quarry. The scattered remains at the quarry reveal that they worked simultaneously on all stages of production until the end of the expedition. First suitable blocks were lifted out of the lake muds and shaped roughly to the final dimensions of the statues. These blocks were transferred to a loading ramp by a process of levering and wedging and then lowered from the top of the ramp onto a sledge into trackways cut into the mud below the ramp.

Excavations also show that in the Old Kingdom the site was supported by wells, and brewing and baking were conducted in an area near Quartz Ridge. The surface into which the sledge tracks and wells were cut also

FIGURE 3.10 Loading ramp for the Cephren diorite Quarry at Gebel al-Asr constructed from striped blocks of the diorite that was used for the statues at Khafra's pyramid at Giza in the north of Egypt

hosted aestivating snails (see Figure 2.1), *Zootechus insularis*, a species that can endure seven years of drought and is known for surviving in museums for years before a period of humidity stimulates them to walk around inside the display cases (e.g. at the British Museum). These small snails are another indicator of the relatively mild climate of the site at the time of Khafra. The most likely route for the egress of the sledges from the site is through the Wadi Toshka, the same spillway that formerly fed the Khargan Basin and into the Nile Valley in Nubia, an area now flooded by Lake Nasser.

The quarries were reused during the Middle Kingdom but workshops and storerooms were by then tightly clustered around a settlement at Quartz Ridge, with a large number of storage jars being used by the expedition. Even though a bird's nest found amongst these jars, sealed by later sand, indicated milder conditions than today, the impression is more of a fully provisioned mission than a seasonal settlement. The Middle Kingdom route to the Nile, to avoid the long way around through the Wadi Toshka, was a donkey trail marked by cairns that made its way to the closest point in the Nile Valley (Bloxham 1998). The material extracted at this period was exclusively for smaller pieces such as bowls and jars and many of the latter are found in Egypt associated with the rite of the 'opening of the mouth', part of the funerary ritual. At Gebel al-Asr, laminated wind-blown sand, characteristic of the early phase of sand release from the Sahara, encapsulates the Middle Kingdom remains, even though, in the north at Giza, it had already started to enclose buildings of the earlier periods in the time of Khafra.

In summary, during the further aridification of the Sahara, the wadis that impinged upon the Nile added sand and gravel to the Nile Valley, raising the floodplain. The new sediment also infilled marshes and channels and gradually reduced them to a few main arteries. Although the channels still meandered, they were less prone to switching than the multiple channels that preceded them. These new stable channels built larger levees, rising 2 metres or more above the surrounding floodplain to become attractive spots for settlement. They were close to the river but safe from the flood. By the same token, in the delta, the previously isolated sand islands (gezirehs) also became more accessible as the channels and marshes between them began to fill. Early inhabitants lived around the shores of the islands, finding a refuge from the flood for their dead and their families during the flood season. Early populations who had earlier made the desert their home and only occasionally visited the Nile had now moved to the cusp of these two habitats. As the Saharan region became more desert and the Nile Valley tamer they were soon to turn their back on the desert entirely.

4

THE DEVELOPMENT OF EGYPT'S
CAPITALS: CONDENSATION OF THE
NILE INTO MEANDERING CHANNELS
WITH INHABITED LEVEES

A S THE SAHARAN AREA DECLINED IN IMPORTANCE, POPULATIONS
settled down to a sedentary existence in the Nile Valley. During the
Old Kingdom, settlements and estate towns were restricted to the safe high
ground of the levees and islands. These levees were long low swells fringing
the Nile and its former channels, and the settlements were strung out along
them and confined to the tops during the flood. As the floodwaters receded,
agricultural and pastoral activity spread out into the surrounding floodplain.
Occasional wetter periods reanimated interest in the deserts, in particular
from mining expeditions, but there was generally insufficient water for permanent residence. The wadi mouths and the nearby desert still supported sufficient drought-tolerant game to act as a hunting range. Eventually, towards
the end of the Old Kingdom, the vegetation died and wind-blown sand
from the Sahara started to drift into the Nile Valley in the north, masking
the topography, infilling channels and creating dune fields over some of the
Nile silts. The blown sand gradually mantled areas further and further to the
south until, by the end of the Middle Kingdom, the whole of Egypt was
blanketed with sand. The sand incursion led to further floodplain rise and
greater consolidation of the delta.

The general trend from the mid-Holocene was one of gradual desiccation as drying commenced in the north and continued southwards (Kuper
and Kröpelin 2006). However, local microclimates and short-range temperature excursions from the general trend meant that the associated landscape changes were not synchronised across Egypt. The evidence discussed
below shows the kinds of landscape changes that affected the Nile Valley as
a result of climate cycling. Broadly, as temperatures rose, the Nile flood was
enhanced, the deserts greened and the floodplain was expanded. Arguably
these changes militated towards a period of population expansion and stability. Conversely, as temperatures fell, desiccation of the deserts and wadis

led to sediment collapse from the wadis into the Nile Valley which, in the context of a lowered flood, narrowed the floodplain and may have led to pressure on the population in terms of reduced food security through loss of territory. Ultimately drifting sand was released from fossil dune fields and overwhelmed many sites across Egypt.

We can thus consider climate cycles as having a number of phases. For a brief amelioration of climate, little more than a blooming of the desert or a few years of rainier weather may occur, but where these cycles extend over hundreds or thousands of years, whole new habitats and ecosystems arise. For example, during the sixth millennium BC in the Kharga Basin (see Chapter 2), lakes refilled and their environs were vegetated with trees, forming a focus for wildlife and a source of grassy food materials that was colonised by hunter-gatherers of the North African Neolithic (Garcea 2006, Bubenzer and Riemer 2007). This ~500-year period of warmer weather produced similar habitats at Nabta Playa, in Kharga and in the Farafra Oasis (Barich et al. 2014). Moreover, the large relict lake beds that formed during the Pleistocene (Haynes et al. 1979, Maxwell et al. 2010) contained muds that could readily flourish with the simple addition of rainwater.

Habitat Hysteresis

Observations of modern habitats in Egypt suggest that climate cycles can be divided into several phases, from flood to famine, which have positive as well as negative impacts upon those living in the area. As temperatures first rise, rainfall, arriving in a desiccated area with no vegetation, may initially cause wadi collapse and, depending upon the severity of the weather, flooding and devastation. The Tempest Stele of Ahmose I, from the opening of the New Kingdom, may record one such disaster with a description of 'corpses floating on the water like skiffs of papyrus' (Ritner and Moeller 2014), although some authors (Polinger et al. 1996) link the events to the eruption of Thera, which caused temporary cooling.

At the same time as increasing local rainfall, warming increases the intensity of the monsoon in Ethiopia and raises the level of the annual summer flood, extending fertile Nile sediments over the flanks of the Nile Valley and impinging upon the mouths of the wadis that meet it. Meanwhile the direct rainfall in the Saharan hinterland fosters the development of vegetation in the wadis, creating additional habitat for game. Although high floods may damage canals, sluices and other irrigation infrastructure, during the agricultural season that follows a high flood, large areas of fresh, wet soil are available. Incidentally, the expansion of the river into old channel beds and

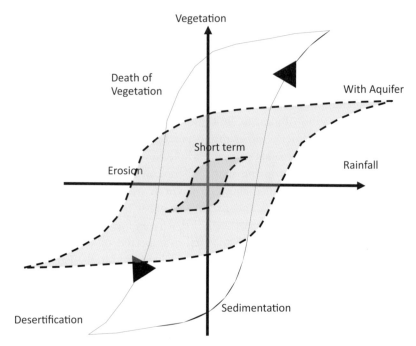

FIGURE 4.1 Diagram to show the effect of a rainy episode on habitat

the refilling of marshes in low ground may, at this stage, lead to a higher risk of waterborne disease, of which bilharzia and malaria are known to be common in Egypt and whose traces are found on ancient burials.

As the climate cycle returns towards drier conditions, lakes and marshes dry, exposing rich sediments that are relatively wet and easily irrigable. Local aquifers are full and can release water back into the sediment. The risk of disease ameliorates as marshes start to dry, and the dry sunny conditions ensure that a bumper harvest can be obtained. However, if drier conditions persist, the flood intensity is reduced, aquifers become depleted, desert wells and vegetation are exhausted and productivity falls again, with the resultant pressure on the now expanded population. Salts dissolved in the water of playa lakes and their residual waterholes become concentrated and the water source may become bitter and sterile. Figure 4.1 shows how a period of rainier weather first generates flooding and sedimentation followed by the development of vegetation (solid loop). As the rainy season or seasons are reduced, vegetation dies, releasing sediment during rainfall followed eventually by a return to desert. For a single wet season (small dotted loop) grasses and shrubs may become established but, in some cases in the Sahara, wetter climate persisted for up to five hundred years (large dotted loop) when lakes and forests became established. Both vegetation and groundwater reservoirs buffer the effects of climate change, meaning that vegetation can survive for some time after the rains cease.

Within this cycle of greening and drying, the time most advantageous to human habitation is when drying begins. If desiccation continues, however, the following stage is insufficient flooding for irrigation and fertilisation, coupled with eventual collapse of the wadi beds, narrowing the floodplain further. The sediments around Luxor provide an excellent example of the magnitude of these changes. Relics of early Holocene Nile silts are 30m above the current level of the floodplain. At the time of deposition water must have penetrated far into the wadi mouths of the Theban Mountain and, given the additional rainfall in the massif at that time, the wadis were an excellent habitat with access to the largely aquatic Nile Valley. For example, rock art and a settlement in the Theban Mountain near Luxor (Litherland 2015) demonstrates the use of rock shelters during the Pre-Dynastic period. Dryer periods with intermittent rain, for example the rain storms recorded during the nineteenth dynasty (Dorn 2016), have however led to the deposition of around 2 m of wadi cobbles over the formerly vegetated soils that underlie them.

The shift of Memphis, near modern Cairo, from the desert edges into the Nile Valley during the early Old Kingdom is a case in point. Early Dynastic remains in the Memphis area survive to the west on the desert edge, adjacent to the Saqqara Plateau (Jeffreys 1985) and to the east on the Helwan Palaeofan. Whether there had been earlier remains from these periods or not within the Nile floodplain, by now they would have been expunged by the subsequent passage of the river. Signs of habitation within the valley start to be seen during the Old Kingdom, restricted to and stretching along the levees of the now emerging river channels (Jeffreys and Tavares 1994) and upon islands. However, the Nile was meandering (see Chapter 8 for more details) and migrating eastwards. As it migrated, the river spawned new islands, each in turn bonding to the western bank of the river while new islands formed to the east. Pedro Goncalves (Cambridge University PhD dissertation in preparation) shows that Memphis developed as an archipelago but, as channels dried up or were blocked by human activity, the site continued to accrete.

It is difficult, however, to dissociate the earliest periods of the settlement towards the western side of the Nile Valley from the earlier sites upon the Saqqara plateau to the west. Significant monuments in this area include Early Dynastic cemeteries, mastaba tombs and, during the 3rd Dynasty, the prototype pyramid, the Step Pyramid of Djoser. Following Djoser's innovation at the dawn of the Old Kingdom, other pyramids were built at Saqqara and a little further north at Abusir. Although many pyramids, causeways and valley temples survive from the Old Kingdom there is little evidence for the settlements in which those who died had lived. Some exploratory work by David Jeffreys with the Survey of Memphis encountered the remains of Early Dynastic settlements at the base of the cliffs at Saqqara, but a mixture of the high-water table, encroaching sand and subsequent building meant that the extent and development of these settlements could not be explored (Jeffreys and Bunbury 2005). Much as we know about the activities pertaining to death in the Saqqara area, the location of settlements of life in this area is less well understood. (For more details of the later development of Memphis, see Chapter 8.)

The increasing channelisation of the Nile during this period, with its tendency to construct natural levees, also blocked the mouths of the fringing wadis to create natural lakes and marshes. These were, in some cases, artificially re-wet or maintained as lakes, of which the Lake of Abusir is an example. To the north of Saqqara at Abusir, Paul Nicholson (Nicholson et al. 2013) encountered Early Dynastic material on an ancient river levee towards the western limit of the floodplain. The river levee in this area cuts across and effectively forms a natural dam to the mouth of the wadi. Boreholes sunk through the sediments in this area (Earl 2010) showed that there had been a lake in the area during the Old Kingdom. Whether this lake had been refreshed with water channelled deliberately from the Nile is unclear but, after a period of abandonment, a marsh had been created in the same area during the New Kingdom. One inference is that the natural lake bed had been deliberately re-flooded in order to breed some of the two million sacred ibis required for mummification and interment in the ibis galleries of the Saqqara plateau (Nicholson 2013). The extent of these ancient lakes can be mapped in the Memphis/Abusir area by inspection of the location of date groves, since the date palm thrives in the 6 m or more of damp soil that is provided by the ancient lake beds and abandoned channels (Figure 4.2).

Climate curves suggest that from the end of the Old Kingdom until the beginning of the New Kingdom, conditions remained dry in Egypt, particularly in the north, although Nadine Moeller (personal communication) notes that in the area of Edfu the hiatus experienced further north is absent. The net result of these climate shifts was to detach life in the delta from life in Upper Egypt and during the late Middle Kingdom and the Second Intermediate period there was a gradual loss of Egyptian control of the delta area, which was taken over by the Hyksos, literally the 'rulers

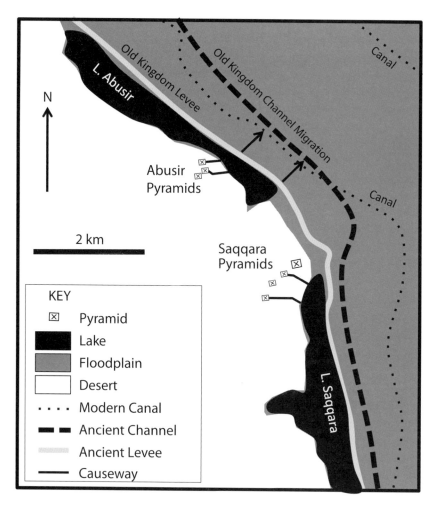

FIGURE 4.2 Map of small marginal lakes in the Abusir area reconstructed by Erin Earl (2010); although formed naturally during the Old Kingdom and used to serve the valley temples of the Saqqara and Abusir pyramid fields, the lakes were renewed during the New Kingdom

of foreign countries'. Cultural links between the delta and the Nile Valley survived with 'Egyptians' from the Theban region seasonally hiring delta land for cattle husbandry, as we understand from the account of the soldier Ahmose (Petty 2014), but essentially the Egypt of the south became a region separated from the north.

The drying of the Saharan region, with concomitant loss of vegetation, exposed sediments in the area to erosion by the north-western trade winds that intensified as tropical weather systems retreated south. Kröpelin et al. (2008) in their study of sediments in Lake Yoa, Chad showed, from the arrival of Mediterranean pollen types in their lake sediments, that these winds had been fully established across the region by Roman times. As today, annual seasonal variations continued and there were warmer and cooler periods as global temperature varied; however, the general trend remained one of gradual drying and intensification of the trade winds with time.

Freshly released sand, deposited during previous dry periods as dunes, began to be remobilised and spread across Egypt into large dune systems (Embabi 2004). At Saqqara, Abusir and Giza sand started to flow into the Nile Valley and buried a number of sites, particularly along the western flank of the Nile canyon, downwind of the Sahara. In Middle Egypt (near Antinoupolis, Verstraeten et al. 2017), sand dunes also encroached onto the floodplain. Similarly, a rapid rise in floodplain level detected at Dashur (Alexanian et al. 2011) and sand deposition recorded in votive jar deposits alongside the causeway tunnel of the Bent Pyramid demonstrate the dramatic effect that the fresh sand had in masking topography, encroaching into the floodplain and adding sediment load to the Nile.

The additional sand led to another episode of floodplain narrowing and rise. Some sand was flushed through the Nile system and added to the delta (Woodward et al. 2007), infilling marshes and pools and transforming the local network of channels from many small ones to a radiating set of distributary rivers (Pennington et al. 2016). A substantial pool at Merimde (Rowland and Tassie 2014) was filled with several metres of sand during this period, changing the environment from one of islands dominated by water to one of a few channels dominated by land. The growth of Memphis as an entrepôt may partly reflect the changing architecture of the delta channel network and the increase in land area for pastoralism in the delta (for more details of changes in the delta see Chapter 7). The addition of sand to the Nile Valley also accelerated the process of channel and levee formation.

Ultimately drying, which began in the north during the late Old Kingdom and, over the following millennium, swept southwards across the Saharan region, focussed a diverse population from the fertile realm into the Nile Valley. Brief periods of amelioration or advances in technology, such as the introduction of the camel in Roman times, meant rediscovery and, in some cases, redevelopment of ancient sites, but in general civilisation was focussed into the long but narrow strip of the Nile Valley. The influx of sand from the desert meant that the Nile Valley, as well as being more densely populated, was also changing rapidly.

5

CLIMATE CHANGE AND CRISIS: DIFFERING VIEWS OF DEVOLUTION ACROSS THE FIRST INTERMEDIATE PERIOD

DECENTRALISATION OF EGYPTIAN CIVILIZATION DURING THE late Old Kingdom is often attributed to the influx of sand from the – by then – arid Sahara. The sand poured over the western cliffs into the Nile Valley, overwhelming Old Kingdom sites like Saqqara and Giza in the north. The new sediment also contributed to the consolidation of the delta and a rapid rise and narrowing of the Nile floodplain. With the human population concentrated in the Nile Valley and increasingly dependent upon irrigation and agriculture of the floodplain, large population centres started to grow, in particular around Memphis. Many important sites became concentrated in the north of the country around the area that is now Cairo. Old Kingdom monuments include around 120 large pyramids, which spread from Abu Rawash in the north to Maidum and Hawara in the south.

The death of the Sahara, and the demise of its tropical vegetative cover, also stimulated changes in the Egyptian delta from a marsh-rich environment to one with a dryer landscape and more tightly focussed distributary channels (for more detail on the delta see Chapter 7). With populations increasingly dependent upon the Nile and the produce of a narrow floodplain, space was at a premium. It was also, as we shall see, part of a constantly changing environment where deposition and erosion were active. It followed that the safest place to bury the dead was in the fringing wadis or the cliffs of the Nile Canyon, and large mortuary complexes developed along the edges of the Nile Valley. Ironically it is the records of these necropolises that tell us more about the living than the place where they lived, since the Nile floodplain, like a magnetic tape, has been overwritten by subsequent events.

As populations collected along the banks of the Nile where the floodplain broadens north of Aswan, commerce and trade by boat became more important, requiring considerable resources from the Levant as suitable boat-building timber was not available in Egypt. At some point,

Hierakonpolis was displaced as the capital and moved to the north, which was favoured by Old Kingdom pharaohs and the visionaries of the 'Age of the Pyramids'. At this time, it is also clear that Memphis (Bunbury et al. 2017) was advantageously situated in an area where increasing resource was available from the maturing landscape of the delta (see Chapter 7). The Old Kingdom flourishing ended when power was no longer centralised across Egypt. The following period is known as the First Intermediate Period, which is said to stretch from 2200 BC to 2000 BC (see Chapter 6). Many of the sand incursions into the Nile Valley were documented by the geologist and anthropologist Fekri Hassan. His work concludes that climate change in Egypt was abrupt and hence its effect dramatic. Many events, such as failing floods and civil unrest, were ascribed by Hassan to a single dramatic climatic change at the end of the Old Kingdom, coinciding with the First Intermediate Period (Hassan 1996).

The rapid incursion of sand is particularly well documented by the accumulations at Dashur. We know from the archaeological sections at Dashur that sand release was rapid from the late 4th Dynasty until the 12th Dynasty (Alexanian et al. 2012); 5.5 m of sand were redeposited by the wind over the tunnel constructed for Sneferu. Contemporary with the Valley Temple (early 4th Dynasty of Old Kingdom) a mud-brick tunnel was constructed which led down to a rectangular enclosure in the wadi that ultimately gave on to the Nile Valley (Alexanian et al. 2010). The tunnel was built on the shattered stone or tafla of the desert surface and did not incorporate sand into its walls. The team also suggested that the builders of the pyramid complex lived in a settlement, now buried, that was just outside the wadi mouth at a considerably lower level of the floodplain.

Soon after the construction of the tunnel (Figure 5.1), votive jars (c. 2589 BC) were laid against the outside of it, and not long after this, sand sifting out of the desert started to accumulate. Votive jars continued to be deposited, revealing that the rates of sand accumulation were rapid during the Old Kingdom. By the end of the Old Kingdom the tunnel and the rectangular enclosure and much of the earlier topography of the wadi were completely buried by sand. Sand accumulation continued at a slower rate and a causeway between the Valley Temple and the Nile Valley was constructed. The Nile Valley is visible from its trees in the background of the picture. The causeway was made of blocks quarried from the Valley Temple during the New Kingdom and shows the level to which sand had accumulated at that time. Since then a relatively small amount of additional sand (c. 2 m) has accumulated. After all this sand accumulation, the tunnel and the mud brick of the rectangular enclosure were so deeply buried that they were only

FIGURE 5.1 Mud-brick tunnel leading from the Valley Temple of the Bent Pyramid at Dashur

identified from geophysical measurements intended to reveal the location of a causeway.

Both the evidence from Dashur and other sites as well as the literary genre of lamentation that appeared from the Middle Kingdom suggest noticeable climate change around the end of the Old Kingdom, but the debate as to how quickly these events happened remains alive today. Although the evidence from the capital zone suggests one single dramatic period of climate change for all Egypt, as detailed by Hassan, excavations further to the south reveal that the changes were more sweeping and delayed in the south by nine hundred or more years. From her observations at Edfu, Moeller (2005) supports the idea that there was a gradual degradation of landscape sweeping southwards across Egypt from the end of the Pre-Dynastic and continuing until the New Kingdom (3100–1070 BC). Borehole studies from Chad and other settlements (Kuper and Kröpelin 2006, Kröpelin 2008) also describe a smoother transition, caused by ecological zones retreating southward.

Other nearby sites like Abusir also record evidence of sand incursion, with Early Dynastic sites there covered by sand (Jeffreys and Tavares 1994).

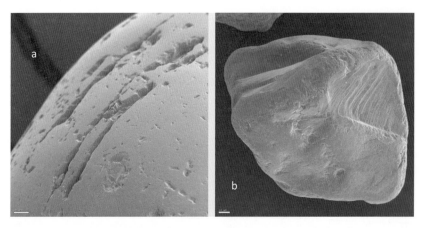

FIGURE 5.2 Microscope images of sand grains from Memphis (scale bar 20 nm)

For Memphis, Ying Qin, a geology masters student at Cambridge University, showed from the microscopic morphology of sand grains in sandbanks associated with the ancient city of Memphis (Figure 5.2) that they had only been transported a short distance in water after being blown in from the desert (Cambridge University unpublished dissertation 2007). Microscopic analysis of the rounding of the left-hand grain is typical of erosion and transport by wind, while the right-hand grain shows a few shell-shaped chips, characteristic of water transport and deposition. The shape of the majority of grains at Memphis is dominated by wind-blown rounding. The addition of so much sand to the Nile channel meant that it became very active with many channels and sandbanks while it flushed out the additional sediment. Evidence for the rapidly changing environment appears in many strands of evidence.

The First Intermediate Period in ancient Egyptian history is often looked upon as a dark time – a time of adjustment, chaos and political disorder in stark contrast to the wealth and harmony that existed during the Old Kingdom. Much of Middle Kingdom literature corroborates this view by recalling apocalyptic events, failing floods and civil unrest, as do some more recent authors (Hassan 1996) who attribute many lines of evidence for climate change to events during this period. The First Intermediate Period coincided with low floods, seen in evidence from the Qarun Lake Levels of the Faiyum Depression; continued encroachment of sand brought forth by winds in the Sahara; tropical trees displaced by Sahel-type trees and decay of sporadic vegetation; and rainfall below 150 mm/yr (Kröpelin et al. 2008). Coupled with observations of sands (Goncalves, Survey of Memphis

Cambridge University PhD dissertation in preparation) and flood deposits around Memphis towards the end of the Old Kingdom, we may posit that the addition of abundant sediment to the Nile generated an increased number of islands in the river and produced a period of enhanced floodplain rise. The additional sediment also hastened the maturation of the delta, accompanied by movement of the delta head northwards (see Chapter 7), as supported by the work of Pryer (2011) and Bunbury et al. (2017).

The First Intermediate Period was also a time of political change, with a number of local rulers rising to power, and Early Middle Kingdom literature (c. 2000 BC) appears to record apocalyptic events. If this period was indeed one of environmental change, then conflict between inhabitants is a natural consequence. As resources decline or habitats shift there is a stimulus for developments in technology as people are forced to adapt and try new things; creativity and progress go hand in hand with hardship as tribes discover new frontiers and build new towns. As life became increasingly difficult for Egyptians, so their rulers found their tight grip on power weaken and the ancient hegemony of the one single pharaoh, overseeing and ruling over his people, declined. Regional rulers, nomarchs, filled the power vacuum left by the old, departing, centralised kingdom. Memphis remained an important town in the north, overseeing a growing area of agricultural land in the delta region and forming close trading connections with the eastern Mediterranean. At the same time, a new capital arose in the south at Thebes which could command an expansion of empire to the south into the Nubian region and the Kingdom of Kush (see Chapter 9). Records and early forms of literature paint a powerful, and often moving, picture of climatic change and its subsequent role in defining a way of life for many ancient Egyptians.

It is unsurprising, then, that the ancient Egyptians, now becoming so inevitably bound to the Nile, became interested in measuring and recording flood heights and taking measures, both secular and spiritual, to control the river. Their preoccupation with Nile behaviour can be seen from the earliest writings from the Pre-Dynastic onwards. From the beginning of the Old Kingdom (2700 BC), efforts were directed towards recording and predicting Nile levels year on year. Observations of the peak height of the flood were essential to the management of irrigation systems and to the setting of the tax levels for the forthcoming harvests. The extensive tax records of the Wilbour Papyrus from the New Kingdom demonstrate how complex land registration and taxation systems had become by that time. Other literature, also from the same period, provides ample evidence of the changes in Nile levels at the time and the lengths to which ancient Egyptians went to monitor and control its flow.

Beyond these records of the annual cycle, an early Middle Kingdom text, the 'Prophecy of Neferti', suggests that there was already a perception of longer-range environmental change, while by the time of Herodotus (c. 440 BC) there were reports of lake levels in the Faiyum being different from those in the time of King Moeris, nine hundred years earlier. In fact, one could argue that the Egyptian 'media' were as preoccupied with Nile behaviour as Britons are with the weather. Years of abundant floods are confirmed in the poem 'Instructions of Amenemhat', which details a conversation between a dead pharaoh and his son, written in the time of the Middle Kingdom. It tells of excess of food and the success of harvests:

> It was I who brought forth grain, the grain god loved me,
> the Nile adored me from his every source;
> one did not hunger during my years, did not thirst;
> they sat content with all my deeds, remembering me fondly;
> and I set each thing firmly in its place.
>
> Translated Parkinson (1991)

Similarly, the early Middle Kingdom Tale of Sinuhe captures the landscape in prose for all eternity (translated in Lichtheim 1973). A scribal study text in the Egyptian school system, the tale was much loved and much copied. The story, presented in the form of a tomb biography, showed a model subject to the boys, who copied and recopied it. Sinuhe is writing at the end of his life, much of which was spent in exile. He explains why he fled, re-swears his allegiance to the king and begs to be allowed to return to his homeland before he dies. Although the story is widely held to be fiction, as with the best fiction it is set in the real landscape (Figure 5.3). The map shows the reconstruction of the landscape at the time that the Tale of Sinuhe was written, with the double channel inferred from auger exploration. From the map, we can reconstruct Sinuhe's supposedly fictional journey in a realistic landscape, revealing that he could cross the minor western Nile branch without a boat while the army continued southwards to the residence but that he was forced to wait until nightfall before he could steal a barge and drift across the larger branch to make good his escape.

In the tale, Sinuhe, a loyal retainer, is in the Wadi Natrun to the north-west of Memphis where he overhears that the old king has died. Fearing a coup, he flees. By the time that he realises that his actions are rash he has already incriminated himself as disloyal so, wading across a river channel, the Maaty, he hides in a bush near Memphis and waits for nightfall. The army, in the meantime, is safely out of the way, marching south to the Residence at Lisht (which places the original story in the Middle Kingdom). Sinuhe creeps out

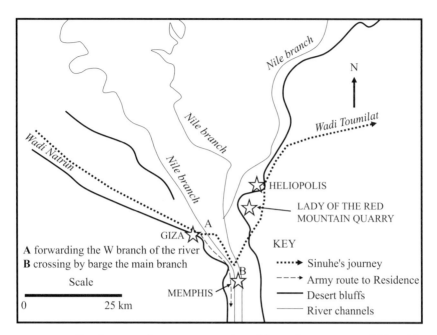

FIGURE 5.3 Sketch map to show a reconstruction of the environment around Memphis at the time of the composition of the Tale of Sinuhe

and, under the cover of darkness, steals a barge from Cattle Quay. Drifting across the Nile, blown by the west wind, he makes good his escape through the Sinai into the Levant. Early translators (Goedicke 1957) struggled with the landscape of Sinuhe since, referencing modern maps, they found that only some of his movements corresponded with real topography. Not least, there is currently only one channel in the Memphis area, whereas Sinuhe seems to cross two. However, by using the work of Lutley (2008) and others to reconstruct the riverine landscape in the Middle Kingdom, Bunbury and Jeffreys (2011) are able to show that in the Middle Kingdom there were two channels: the minor western channel (presumably the easily crossed Maaty) and a larger main channel that required the theft of the barge. It is perhaps a token of the rapidly changing landscape in the Nile Valley that the capital was also particularly mobile at this time and included a Middle Kingdom palace south of the earlier and later centres at Lisht, mentioned in Sinuhe's tale.

In addition to the textual evidence, other evidence from animal remains in owl pellets shows that, during the Old Kingdom, those deposited in the tombs of Saqqara were those of owls that had dined on damp-loving species

of mice and frogs/toads. By the Middle Kingdom owl diets had changed
to one of aridity-tolerant species, such as gerbils and desert toads (Pokorny
et al. 2009). In addition to the fauna, the flora of the desert also suffered and
was dried out. Now that the roots no longer protected the sandy wadi beds
from erosion and the leaves no longer sheltered the sand from the erosive
power of a cloud burst, water and sand rushing down the valley could sweep
away large quantities of sediment as long as there were still rainstorms. With
time, even the rainstorms failed and, although erosion slowed down, being
restricted to wind erosion or deflation, people turned their backs on the
desert. It is interesting to speculate whether the increasingly poor repu-
tation of the desert god, Seth, once an equal if opposite partner of Horus,
was related to increasingly negative attitudes to the now denuded deserts.
Figure 5.4 shows a late image of the king destroying Seth, by now a diminu-
tive hippopotamus, from the Ptolemaic Temple of Edfu.

The location of the palace in the Sinuhe story was at Itj-Tawi, generally
thought to be in the area of Lisht, an ancient capital of Egypt, to the south of
Cairo. However, the precise location of the palace was unknown as a result
of the rapidly changing landscapes of the Middle Kingdom (Figure 5.5).
Shifting sands meant that the river channels were rapidly migrating and the
head of the delta was seemingly also mobile. In a bid to locate the palace
at Lisht more closely, Sarah Parcak, as part of a BBC project, identified the
area (Sa el-Hagar), from topography and field patterns in satellite imagery,
as the levee of an ancient river channel (Figure 5.2) and the potential site
of the palace. The modern village is close to the early Middle Kingdom
pyramids of Amenemhat I and Senusret I but, as the location of Middle
Kingdom habitations in the area was unknown, the neighbouring ancient
riverbank seemed the most suitable place to explore. The satellite image
reconstruction shows an ancient channel with the areas of investigation
marked by stars, on the basis that they were on the levee and within range
of the pyramid.

To explore further we sank a set of boreholes along the ancient levee
in Area 1 penetrating 5 m of overlying floodplain silt before encountering
worn sherds that belonged to domestic pottery used for storage and as table-
ware during the Middle Kingdom. Further boring reached a sandy bed
containing a rich mixture of ash, charcoal and sherds associated with semi-
precious stone chips, including carnelian and amethyst, which was accompanied by elite pottery from the Middle Kingdom (Bettina Bader, personal
communication). Both stones, particularly amethyst, were prized in jewel-
lery during the Middle Kingdom. Parcak identified the riches, indicated by
the borehole chippings, with the elite workshops of Itj-Tawi, a capital in

FIGURE 5.4 King destroying Seth, from the Ptolemaic Temple of Edfu

the Lisht area (BBC, Egypt's Lost Cities). Borings in the other area (Area 2) encountered a later Graeco-Roman site.

Documentary and architectural evidence can be used to map the way in which the centres of power moved in Egypt's northern capital zone (Figure 5.6). Although in the early Middle Kingdom the palace seems to

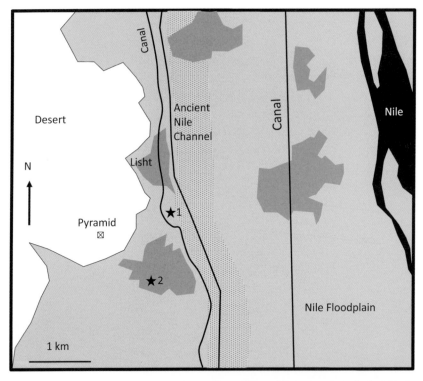

FIGURE 5.5 Map of the area around the modern village of Lisht from which the Nile is far distant

have been located at Lisht, at the same time another Middle Kingdom site to the west of Mit Rahina was also gaining in importance and would ultimately become the city of Memphis. All that remains now of the mighty city of Memphis, the location of a scribal school and where Herodotus based his enquiries in northern Egypt around 440 BC, are mounds. Recent studies by David Jeffreys and Pedro Goncalves with the Survey of Memphis show that the city adapted through its long history. The early western centres spread and parts of the community were established on a number of river levees in the area. Ana Tavares (Bunbury et al. 2017) proposes, therefore, that Memphis was a 'garden city' with fertile irrigated (and flooded) areas between settlements that were restricted to the higher ground. By the New Kingdom, a broader concept of the landscape emerged and Pedro Goncalves postulates that a waning channel of the Nile was dissected to create a new site for the Temple of Ptah that could be accessed from harbours to the south and to the north. It remains a matter of discussion whether the New

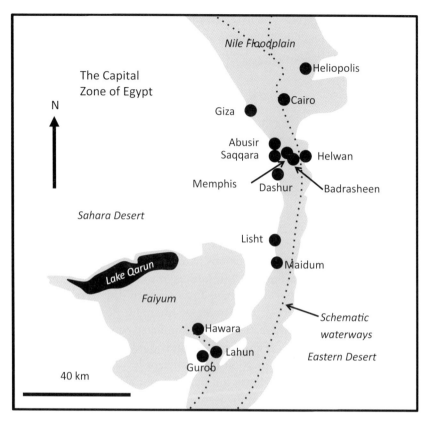

FIGURE 5.6 Sketch map of the capital zone of Egypt showing the main sites of administrative control (see Figure 2.6 for wider area)

Kingdom works at Gurob, further south, directing water from the Bahr Yusuf, the minor western branch of the Nile, into the Faiyum, were partly responsible for the emergence of drier land at Memphis.

A little later, in Ptolemaic times, Ying Qin shows how a new connection to an old channel was excavated, setting the scene for the siege of Memphis as recorded in the Stele of Piye. In the narrative, the attackers cut out all the watercraft from the 'North Harbour' (Parkinson 1991, Bunbury and Jeffreys 2011) and assemble them into a giant floating siege engine, surprising the defenders by storming the eastern harbour walls at dawn. Westerly channels continued to diminish and the main river to migrate eastwards until in the Roman period (Jeffreys 1985) a waterfront wall with nymphaeum was established to the east side of the mounds. To the north-west, perhaps as a result of delta-head migration, a new centre was emerging at Egyptian

Babylon, where a Roman watergate remains today. Memphis waned and fell into ruin, although new villages continued to track the Nile as it moved eastwards.

Slow Retreat of the Desert

Auger research across Egypt confirms the idea that rather than a single dramatic climate change, there was a slow retreat of the tropical grasslands southwards and that desertification of the north was already occurring at some point in the early Old Kingdom. The work of the Egyptian Nile Land and Waterscape Survey has made possible the dating of sand entrainment across Egypt. Auger cores were sunk at a number of sites and analysed (Bunbury et al. 2008), and reveal that polished coarse sand grains were ubiquitous. However, in lower parts of cores sunk at Karnak (Bunbury et al. 2008) and further investigations at Gebel-al-Asr (Shaw et al. 2001) there were no such sand grains. Excavations in the north reveal that there was wind entrainment of sand there first – a view supported by David Jeffreys through his work at the Survey of Memphis (just south of Giza), and similarly at Giza where the earliest laminated sand deposits predate Khafra's settlement there (Figure 5.7). A sandy bank on the Mena House Golf Course indicates the location of an ancient levee of a Nile channel, a precursor of the modern canal, the Bahr Libeini. Geophysical investigation by Glen Dash showed that the feature persists at depth and is therefore likely to be a relic of a much older levee possibly contemporary with the construction of the pyramids.

In the case of Karnak, a site that flourished in the Middle Kingdom, polished sand granules are again common in the upper parts of the site, but the earliest recorded deposits from the Early Eleventh Dynasty (~4050 BP) rest on river sands that are free of polished granules (Bunbury et al. 2008). Observations suggest that the earliest sand entrainment and redeposition in the Nile Valley was earlier than the First Intermediate Period (Alexanian et al. 2010) in the north (Giza/Memphis) but postdated the Middle Kingdom quarries at Gebel al-Asr in the south, which were also operated in the time of Khafra (Shaw et al. 2001).

When the predicted timescales of sand entrainment are compared with the time of sand entrainment recorded in the Lake Yoa core in Chad, there is an increasing gap between sand deposits seen at Gebel al-Asr (about one hundred years), Karnak in the south (about two hundred years) and Giza/ Memphis (around nine hundred years). This is interpreted as further evidence of a slow retreat of the tropical grasslands southwards. By the Middle

FIGURE 5.7 Under cover of a round of golf, Angus Graham and the team investigate a sandy bank that crosses the Mena House Golf Course at Giza

Kingdom, grasslands had retreated as far as Karnak, while even the south of Egypt had become desert by the end of this period. Within this general pattern of retreat of habitat southwards, warmer intervals allowed the deserts to bloom (see Chapter 10).

Essentially, climate change was and always will be a global phenomenon. In ancient Egypt, it proceeded through the Early Dynastic and Old Kingdom with a gradual reduction in the vegetation in the desert and wadis. It was, however, in the First Intermediate Period that the ancient climate change advocates finally found their voice. The perception of climate change and degradation was suddenly lamented. When Egypt was reunified at the beginning of the Middle Kingdom the scholars drew heavily upon Old Kingdom art and writings, which they viewed as products of the golden age of Egyptian civilisation. Perhaps we will never know whether the pyramids were a product of such a golden age or whether they were an attempt, through the agency of the pharaoh, to take control of an increasingly hostile environment. At Balat in the Dakhla Oasis (25°33.46'N, 29°16.14'E), during the reign of Pepi II, the valiant battle against the encroaching sand was lost and the Old Kingdom was brought to a close. Sand grains in borehole sediments mirror this (Bunbury et al. 2008), with an increase in rounded desert sand grains that corresponds to the pattern from the excavations.

It seems that the widespread invasion of the Nile Valley by sand (particularly from the west) was a defining period in ancient Egyptian history. Such events are recorded in the Middle Kingdom literature of the north in the 'Prophecy of Neferti'. This retrospective text, set in the time of Sneferu (c. 2614–2579 BC), was written later in the reign of the Middle Kingdom king Amenemhat I (c. 1976–1947 BC).

> ... Egypt's river shall run dry so that one may walk dry-shod across it;
> They shall seek water for ships to sail on – the river's course is now but dusty land.
> Riverbank shall turn to flood, and water's home shall be the place for shore ...
>
> From the prophecy of Neferti, tr. John L. Foster (2001)

The influx of sand to the northern capitals reduced their importance, although Memphis still remained a key town at the head of the delta. The dawn of the Middle Kingdom saw a rise in importance of Karnak further to the south, a town that would also encounter difficulties with changing landscape due to the rapid climatic oscillations of the New Kingdom. To the north, the delta was increasingly well consolidated and provided excellent grazing for cattle, but control of it gradually shifted to rulers from other lands.

6

ISLANDS IN THE NILE

THE INFLUX OF SAND INTO THE NILE VALLEY AND DELTA STARTED to change the character of the river in the valley. Many more islands and sandbanks were formed and some dune fields encroached upon the Nile silts, particularly to the western side of the valley. The landscape effects of this were threefold: a more rapid reduction in the amount of marsh in the delta, an increase in sediment in the Nile spawning more sandbanks in the river and, perhaps most interestingly, a rapid migration of the delta head northwards, where the distributaries start to divide.

Laurence Pryer (2011) proposed that the delta head had moved southwards and later northwards, with the locations of the pyramids tracking the apparent position of the delta head. Pryer's model suggests that the most southerly location of the delta head was at Maidum during the Middle Kingdom (the early second millennium BC) but that after that it migrated northwards again. Thus, the known phases of intense activity at Memphis coincide with these dates, when the city was in closest proximity to the delta head. This is being further explored by Pedro Goncalves (Cambridge University PhD dissertation in preparation). The delta head is a strategic point to control river traffic between Upper Egypt and the delta since all distributaries can be monitored by a single settlement.

The close dependence of populations on the Nile meant that every twist and turn of the channel became a matter of importance to the residents. Build your temple on the outer bend of the river and erosion and destruction will result. Conversely, on the inside of the bend, sandbanks constantly accumulate, silting harbours and rendering the river more distant. The best way to hedge your bets was to found your settlement on an island. Study of recent islands and the way in which they are used by farmers or brickmakers sheds insight on the archaeological remains that we find associated with ancient islands. For an example of the development and capture of a recent island see Badrasheen (Chapter 10); for the uses of modern islands

at Luxor see the Appendix; and for a detailed study of the sediments typically produced by an island in the Nile see Al-Zaniyah Island (also in the
Appendix). In general, it can be said that the lifespan of an island is only
around a century, no more than a few generations, and the consistency with
which farms and temples are located on these island environments suggests
that folk memory of the way that islands behave informed the location of
new developments.

Archaeological evidence for channel migration and island formation and
capture is supplemented by more recent cartographic and pictorial evidence.
This type of change was beautifully illustrated by David Roberts (1796–
1864) in his 1838 illustrating tour of Egypt and the Holy Land. Roberts
painted Luxor Temple from the south-east showing a channel in the fore-
front. The channel that he painted has now been infilled and used for the
construction of the Winter Palace Hotel. In another example, an extensive
borehole survey of the Karnak temples (Bunbury et al. 2008) suggested that
similar processes had occurred there.

Much debate has focussed on the rate at which various changes in the
Nile Valley occur and these have been calculated by a number of academics
at a number of different localities. Hekekyan's early study at Memphis was
ostensibly to work out the rate of vertical aggradation of the Nile floodplain.
An approximate mean rate of aggradation is around 1m/millennium. The
long time span is given to emphasise that the rate is not constant, thus in one
year no new sediment may be deposited or a large amount, c. 10–15 cm, may
be deposited by one annual flood cycle, depending on the dynamics of the
river floodplain. The addition of human detritus raises this rate and in this
way many sites have persisted (including Karnak and Memphis) by rising at a
greater rate than the surrounding floodplain to form a kom (or tell) and thus
ensuring that the community remains dry during the flood season. These
koms are sufficiently elevated that many can be seen on digital elevation
models (DEM) of the Nile floodplain.

Although the early research was dominated by discussion of the rate of
floodplain rise, recent interest has shifted to the lateral migration of the Nile
channel. The Nile is a large river set in a sandy, easily eroded bed that rests
within a rocky canyon running through the Sahara Desert. As the river rises
after rainfall, the water initially accelerates, becoming erosive as it picks up
and carries larger and larger grains of sediment. Eventually the water, now
loaded with sediment, decelerates, dropping and distributing the sediment as
it flows. As the water in the centre of the channel is fast-flowing, it tends to
acquire sediment that it then drops towards the sides of the channel where
the current is slower. This process creates levees, elevated banks that are up to

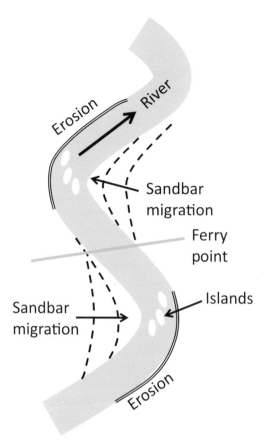

FIGURE 6.1 Schematic diagram to show how rivers meander and where islands form in the channel

2 m high on the Nile main channel. These levees, broad swells up to 200 m wide, may persist for many hundreds of metres along the length of the river. Levees may also dam the entrances to side wadis or spillways and, after some further floodplain rise, be overtopped to form a lake, as we saw in the case of Abusir (see Chapter 4).

Slight curves in the channel mean that the current flows asymmetrically and therefore preferentially erodes the outside of any bends that form while depositing sand, as sandbars, on the inside of the bend and within the channel (Figure 6.1). In many meandering rivers, the classic example being the Mississippi, these meander bends become more and more looped until the narrow neck of land is cut through. Next the channel takes the short way through the cut while the abandoned meander forms an oxbow lake. Dufton (2008) showed that, as the Nile is constrained by its canyon, it cannot ever reach sufficient sinuosity for this process to form oxbow lakes. However, meander bends are common and are constantly migrating outwards and downstream across the valley. When the bend reaches the edge of the valley, which is difficult to erode, it becomes flattened and eventually a new bend migrating in the opposite direction is formed. Maps of migrating bends made for the Memphis floodplain by Katy Lutley give the impression that they 'bounce' off the canyon walls. Former abandoned levees of the river are seen as low swells in the floodplain and may be preferred as sites for occupation. These relic swells are also a couple of metres high and several hundred metres long.

The rate of river migration is sometimes enhanced by island formation and capture, as described by David Jeffreys and the Survey of Memphis at Badrasheen. Their study revealed the pace of change of islands and the amenities that they offer to their residents. During the early twentieth century, a sandy island formed in the Nile bed at Badrasheen, east of the ancient ruins of Memphis. The ownership of the new island was immediately disputed, with communities on both sides of the Nile claiming it as theirs. However, in due course the island bonded itself to the west bank and became de facto a part of Badrasheen. During the 1940s the island had a minor channel, partly blocked to the west, with the main Nile flowing east of it. The resultant mud was put to profitable use by the enterprising inhabitants who built a brick works on the minor branch of the channel to the west of the island. The quiet harbour created by the partly blocked waterway was an ideal place to load the bricks, ready for transportation. By the 1970s the island had lengthened and the minor channel had begun to infill, a process that by 2000 had been completed with the final phase of the infill consolidated by landfill.

Katy Lutley, who made one of the first analyses of Nile migration in the Giza/Memphis floodplain (see also the capital zone case study in Chapter 10), showed that the Nile had migrated over much of the floodplain in the past five thousand years (Lutley and Bunbury 2008, Bunbury et al. 2009 and Figure 6.2). While complex, the diagram indicates how the Nile can have migrated across the whole floodplain during the period of habitation and that the delta head of the Nile was further south in the past than in the present. Lutley's study was largely theoretical and did not determine the precise position of the Nile in space and time but indicates the type of geometry and migration rates that we should expect for any site in the Nile floodplain. She determined that the general rate of migration is around 2,000 m/millennium, with a maximum so far recorded of 9,000 m/millennium where

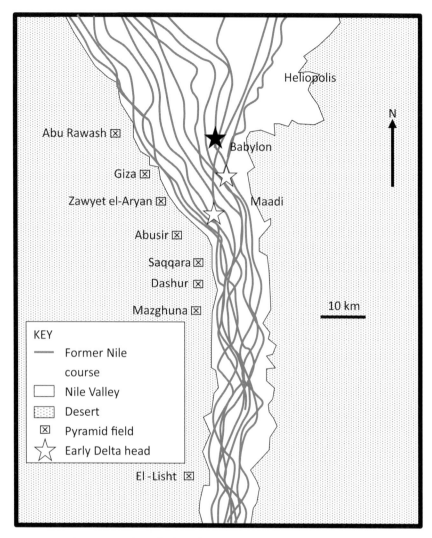

FIGURE 6.2 Diagram to show the best-fit migrations of the Nile in the Giza area over the last 5,000 years (redrawn from Lutley and Bunbury 2008)

island formation and capture are included. From these rates of lateral migration, we see that they exceed the rate of vertical aggradation of 1 m/millennium by three to four orders of magnitude. Thus, when considering the effect of landscape change on a site, the effect of channel migration is likely to have been larger than floodplain aggradation. Fortunately, since there are no tributaries to the Nile in Egypt, the rates of river processes are roughly consistent throughout the whole of the country, making interpretation by the archaeologist relatively straightforward.

In some places, the Nile floodplain is up to 10 km wide, while in others it narrows to the width of the Nile channel such as at Aswan and at Gebel Silsila. Where the river cuts through rocks like those at Gebel Silsila there is no migration, while in other wide floodplains, such as at Memphis, migration across the whole plain is possible. There is an intermediate case where the floodplain is narrow (<2 km) and the river channel, which is around 500 m wide, therefore has little room to migrate. Historically places with this morphology commonly show persistent settlement and may be strategically important since the river is constrained to remain near to the community, for example at Armant where the Nile appears to flip from one side to the other of a central island (Figure 6.3). These points are typically strategic since any settlement can guarantee contact with the river regardless of its migration. The example here is around the tomb of the First Intermediate Period nomarch Ankhtifi. Other examples include Aswan and Asyut, both towns of antiquity that have persisted.

Nile migration of this type seems to have affected many sites in Egypt, including Edfu where the Nile channel has moved across the valley since the area was first inhabited during the Pre-Dynastic period. In fact, it could be reasonably said that, unless the Nile is known to have been restricted by either bedrock (such as at Gebel Silsila) or monuments and revetment (e.g. at Karnak), it should be assumed to have migrated at a mean rate of around 2 km/millennium with up to 9 km/millennium possible. In practice, as the amount of water in the Nile was highly seasonal, until the construction of the Aswan (High) Dam in the late nineteenth century, migration rates were probably rapid during the flood season, Akhet (from July until October); modest during the agricultural season, Perut, which followed the recession of the flood (broadly from November until February); and negligible during the dry season, generally early May to early September.

We know from images on the mace head of the King Scorpion (around 3100 BC), breaching the banks of the water channels with his hoe (Figure 6.4), that water management was an important function in ancient Egypt. The floodplain could be divided into basins that were irrigated in turn to produce crops and, as is the way of all things, taxes. By the New Kingdom, the extensive taxation records of the Wilbour Papyrus (Antoine 2017) reveal that a variety of types of arable land were recognised, each with a characteristic taxation rate. The basin divides (*gisr*), built up to manage the process of irrigation, also acted as roadways that could be kept above the flood level. The

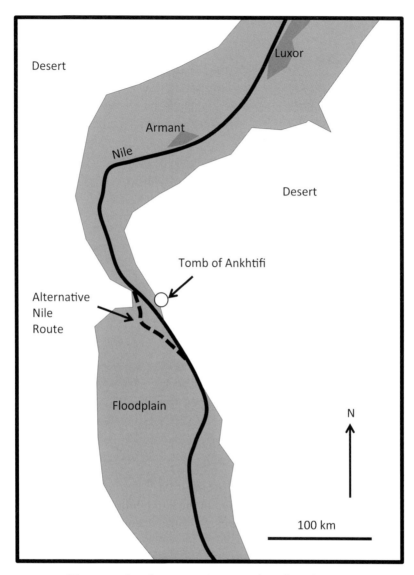

FIGURE 6.3 Diagram to show how, at certain points where the Nile canyon narrows, the river is constrained to flow through a relatively narrow gap

roadways are often associated with canals and have preserved ancient agricultural topographies when silt, accumulating in the channel, was dredged to raise the roadway. As there was no benefit to moving the basin divides and it entailed a great deal of labour, they were seldom moved unless the changes were part of a larger project. More recently, in Graeco-Roman times (300

FIGURE 6.4 Late Pre-Dynastic king depicted wielding a hoe preparatory to breaching a dyke and thus ceremonially commence irrigation (redrawn from the Narmer Mace Head from Nekhen (Hierakonpolis), now in the Ashmolean Museum)

BC to 800 AD) the half a million documents found at Oxyrhynchus (160 km south of Cairo) and reviewed by Parsons (2007) reveal that the maintenance of reservoir banks and channels was still a major occupation during the dry season. In Middle Egypt, Roman remains, for example the study of Eva Subias et al. (2013), suggest that active management of future watercourses by excavating pilot channels could be undertaken during this period.

Comparison with other unconnected civilisations also demonstrates the key importance of managing water supply systems. For example, the Mississippi River in the USA is a more recent example of the anticipation of imminent flooding by digging of pilot channels intended to become more significant waterways as the water rose and became more powerfully erosive. Mark Twain, Missouri's favoured son and one of America's greatest authors, described the history of this great river delta in his memoirs, *Life on the Mississippi* (1883). Here he recalled that there was specific legislation against pilot cut-offs for meander channels that would divert water away from other settlements. Another example of the complex series of negotiations required to manage water resources comes from the Balinese water temples at Pura Tirta where a multi-tiered system of shrines is still used by priests to control irrigation channels and hence water supply to the surrounding paddy fields (Lansing 2007).

In Egypt, agricultural practices have been conservative since antiquity, for example, farmers still broadcast grain from a shoulder bag. Part of the agricultural infrastructure was the division of land into plots. Each year after the inundation, local landmarks were used to lay out plots, known locally as hods, which were then further subdivided by measuring into fields. The hod and field systems are recorded on the cadastral maps so that they persist today even though the flood does not. In this way, therefore, the hod boundaries often delineate ancient landmarks like levees and embankments as well as being a good location for roadways and canals. Since meander bends usually migrate outwards and gradually downstream, the curvature of the hod boundaries indicates the former movements of the river channel (see Figure 6.5) and can indicate the locations of infilled channels.

The characteristics of migration are seen in the Abydos area (Figure 6.5) where islands form on the bends at A and B and can accelerate the process of migration by island capture. Hod boundaries, shown with thin lines, record the passage of the river, showing that at C, for example, migration is towards the north-west. The relative solidity of the rocky walls of the canyon means that at C the river is straightened and a bend migrating to the south-west is likely to emerge next. Arrows elsewhere indicate the inferred direction of river migration at that point. Note particularly that the Nile cannot be said to be generally migrating towards any particular direction but that migration is a product of local topography and morphology. Although the floodplain at Abydos is relatively wide, it is not sufficient for meander bends to become meander cut-offs leaving oxbow lakes, which are unknown from the Nile Valley.

Koms, often associated with channel levees, can be identified from their pre-motorcar morphology, since the street plans of areas occupied before the construction of the Aswan Dam were laid out in as compact a way as possible to maximise the use of the limited space. In Figure 6.6 we see how street plans observed in satellite images delineate the geometry of the movements of the Nile. Further investigation may reveal more detail and, in the case of augering (see Appendix), provide a sense of the time frame within which the changes occurred. Examples of these techniques in action at Hermopolis, Lisht and at Karnak are described below.

The uses of remote inspection can be illustrated by a study of Hermopolis. The Middle Egyptian city, which has Old and Middle Kingdom roots,

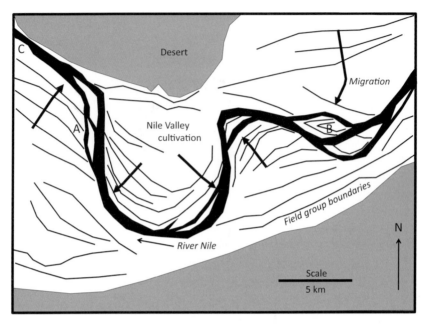

FIGURE 6.5 Diagram (drawn from GoogleEarth satellite images of the Abydos area) showing how the Nile River (black) meanders within the Nile Canyon (white area)

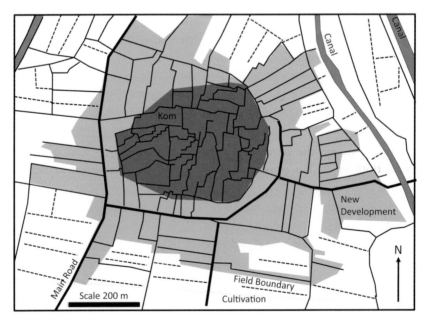

FIGURE 6.6 Pattern of roads and field boundaries redrawn from a typical Egyptian village

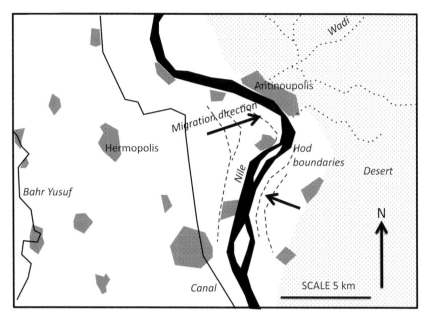

FIGURE 6.7 Map to show the landscape in the Hermopolis–Antinoupolis region

was said in its foundation myth to have been built upon an island in the Nile around 2100 BC, although it is now around 6 km from the main Nile channel (Figure 6.7). The satellite images revealed that the claim to have been founded on an island is entirely reasonable, since mean migration rates would mean that a channel migrating eastwards from Hermopolis would have reached the eastern border of the valley by the time of the foundation of Antinoupolis by Hadrian in 130 AD.

Antinoupolis was also founded on the Nile, to the east of Hermopolis, to commemorate the death of Hadrian's lover Antinous, who drowned there. Both cities, but principally Hermopolis, are mentioned in papyri, many from Oxyrhynchus and the Faiyum, which include deeds, accounts and private correspondence. Consideration of the direction of migration from field patterns after its foundation around 2100 BC, eastwards away from Hermopolis, suggests that it could have reached the location of Antinoupolis by the time of the foundation of that city. The analysis reveals why documents relating to the recruitment of sailors in the town also refer to their transport to the harbour, since the Nile had migrated away from the city by the time of the Roman correspondence (Bunbury and Malouta 2012).

Antinoupolis, a new city adjacent to the desert edge, was undoubtedly in a more accessible position than the ancient city of Hermopolis. However,

Antinoupolis was founded with little land since it is located where the Nile abutted the desert edge, and Heyerdahl's surveys and excavation reveal that many of the monuments were laid out over the desert behind a revetted harbour. The paucity of agricultural land explains why, until the sixth century, many deeds refer to the transfer of land from Hermopolite owners to those from Antinoupolis. The revetments at Antinoupolis mean that the Nile has been unable to migrate away from the city since it was founded. However, the bends to the north and south have started to migrate westwards. Interestingly, deeds from the period after the sixth century tend to be for land transferred from the Antinoupolite population to the Hermopolite one, whose land was, by now, being re-eroded by the Nile.

At Hermopolis we see how the migration of the Nile across the floodplain influenced the locations of cities and bore upon their relative importance in the landscape. Close inspection of the single large site of Karnak in Luxor shows how, at a smaller scale, river migration and island formation also bear upon the development of an individual site. The temples of Karnak in Luxor (Figure 6.8) were built over a long period, starting in the Middle Kingdom, and, allowing for continuity of piety, have continued to the present time, with the shrine of Sheikh Labeib constructed within the temple. The extent of the temples is seen in the aerial photograph taken from the west (Figure 6.8). In the foreground, the First Pylon dominates the centre of the image, with the Sacred Lake formalised by Tutmosis III behind it. The earliest recorded part of the site, known as Tell Karnak and dating to the early First Intermediate Period, is close to the top right-hand corner of the lake. The white strip visible nearby is the staging of the son et lumière. Small white specks in the foreground are the visitors and the tomb of Sheikh Labeib, indicating the continuity of piety, can be seen emerging from the trees in the bottom right-hand corner of the image.

Sedimentary evidence from excavations and boreholes across the area of the temples suggest that the earliest Middle Kingdom limestone temple was constructed on an island in the Nile. The temple was supported by a community located on the banks of the then minor eastern channel (Millet and Masson 2011) and later connected to the mainland as the channel filled in. An *en echelon* sandbar was also occupied with a shrine at Opet to the west, and the Mut Island to the south was the location of another settlement. With time, the minor branch of the Nile was completely filled in and by the late 18th Dynasty (New Kingdom) Akhenaten could construct his temple (*Gmp-aten*) on the infilled channel. That temple was later demolished after Tutankhamun's return from Amarna but its foundations can still be seen in

FIGURE 6.8 Aerial photograph of the temples of Karnak, Luxor

the village to the east of the temple enclosure. Another temple, 'Redford's Temple C', was also constructed within the new flat land provided by the infilled channel.

By the 18th Dynasty the northern part of the island had been stabilised, partly by the addition of rubble to the waterfront, if 10 m of core containing more than 1,000 sherds is taken as a guide. On this newly consolidated land, Tutmosis III (18th Dynasty) constructed his treasury, excavated by Jean Jacquet (1983) and Helen Jacquet-Gordon on the northern part of the site. At the same time Hatshepsut and Tutmosis III also developed a new waterfront with a number of temple courts along the western frontage of the temple. With consolidation of the southern (Mut) island a temple was developed there by Hatshepsut (18th Dynasty); eventually the area between the two was filled with sandbanks and a ceremonial way was constructed between the two sets of temples that can still be seen today. As the land consolidated, new constructions filled the available land and expansion occurred to the west with the construction of a new waterfront (Figure 6.9). This waterfront was equipped with a revetted ramp giving access to the river that flowed, at that time, across the foreground. The ancient waterfront wall can be seen to

FIGURE 6.9 Mansour Boraik's excavation outside the First Pylon at Karnak in 2008

the left of the ramp. With time, the river migrated away from the First Pylon, exposing new ground, and earlier stonework was then reused to create a more gently sloping ramp/slipway that could connect the temple to the new position of the river.

Migration and further development of the waterfront continued into the Roman Period with the construction of a new set of Ptolemaic baths (Figure 6.10) on what had been the earlier waterfront (Boraik et al. 2017). The team photographed working in the excavation augered high-energy river sands containing fresh lumps of the sandstone that was used to make the New Kingdom harbour wall, indicating that it abutted the river at the time of its construction. Later, the Ptolemaic baths, which were constructed over the then defunct waterfront, are visible in the background, in particular the individual washing cells to the top right of the image. A drain serving the baths is visible to the right of the upper figure, cutting through the old New Kingdom wall and passing over later sediment that had accumulated against it.

Hillier showed that the Nile had receded further from the temple towards the west bank but that the river is now migrating eastwards at this point back towards the temple (Hillier et al. 2007). Revetment and erosion management

FIGURE 6.10 Excavation by Salah El-Masekh showing the northwards continuation of the waterfront wall in Figure 6.9

around Luxor means that migration is now very slow through the town. The movements of the Nile around Karnak are summarised in Figure 6.11.

The migrating Nile is a fact of life for those living in the Nile Valley during and since the Old Kingdom, and those who lived or made their

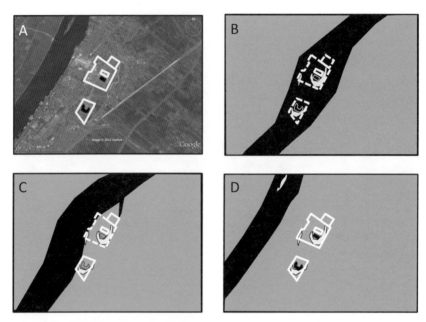

FIGURE 6.11 Maps to show how Karnak, now c. 500 m from the Nile (A), was initially founded on an island (B) (Middle Kingdom temple shown as thick solid lines). As the island extended and consolidated (C) there was further construction during the New Kingdom. With continued Nile migration the river moved away from the complex (D). Pools and the river Nile are shown in black

living near the Nile certainly made the most of the changing landscape. They were enterprising and resourceful, seeking out new opportunities where they could, such as the brickworks at Badrasheen or adapting to new ideas and technologies like those to manage the water cycles and the seasons.

7

THE FLOOD AND THE NEW DELTA

T ODAY APPROXIMATELY ONE THIRD OF EGYPT'S POPULATION LIVES in the delta, one third in the megacity of Cairo and the remaining third in the valley. However, in the past the delta, although a more diverse habitat, was not as extensive as today. The changes in the Saharan region and in the Nile Valley that we have already discussed also affected the delta. Stabilisation of the river channels gradually propagated through the delta moving coastwards, a process that was accelerated by the influx of sand between the Old and New Kingdom (Figure 7.1).

Global sea levels rose at the end of the last ice age 12,500 years ago, meaning that sea-level deltas across the world have evolved in roughly parallel ways (Stanley and Warne 1994 and Figure 7.2). The additional water from the melted ice sheets initially pushed the coastline of the deltas inland. Upstream of the old coast, fresh water from the river system was held back, forming marshes and swamps far inland. The number of distributary branches in this marshy landscape also increased, since channels divide to form distributaries when the base of the main channel reaches sea level. The sea level continued to rise until around 6,000 years ago when the deltas started to recover. With time and sediment supply from the hinterland, the marshes were once again marginalised and the coastline moved offshore again. The rate of sediment supply and the geometry of the sea floor close to the river mouth are the key factors influencing this process (Pennington 2016). Thus, although not exactly in synchrony, the world's sea-level deltas all recovered from inundation by the sea through a series of similar environments. Reports from the informants of Herodotus (c. 440 BC) even tell us that 'the Nile overflowed all Egypt below Memphis'.

Since other deltas are subject to the same processes, we can compare the evolution of the Nile Valley with models derived from more intensively studied deltas such as the Rhine (Makaske 1998, Berendsen and Stouthamer 2001) and the Mississippi (Aslan and Autin 1999). There is a wealth of

FIGURE 7.1 Photograph of the Palestrina Mosaic by kind permission of Délphine Acolat, showing the various activities and landscape of the Nile Delta in the first century BC

geographical data for the Rhine, as data has been collected from 180,000 or more boreholes (Toonen 2013) sunk in the area by generations of geography students. This excellent dataset can be used to understand the new Holocene delta of the Nile which overlaid an earlier Pleistocene delta produced by previous oscillations of sea level during the Pleistocene.

Interpolating data already acquired for the Nile Delta with the theoretical models, Ben Pennington (Pennington et al. 2016) shows that we should expect a very rich habitat for humans in the Early Dynastic (c. 3100–2600 BC) but that, with time, as the delta began to grow again, the level of nutrients available in the environment will decrease (Figure 7.3). The original marshy environments became more and more marginalised to the coastal region of the delta as channels became fewer and better defined, turning into meandering channels. These environments are known as the large-scale crevassing stage (LSC) and the meandering stage (Figure 7.3). During large-scale crevassing (A), rivers are flanked by natural sandy levees which may be breached by the river to create crevasse deposits. There are many islands

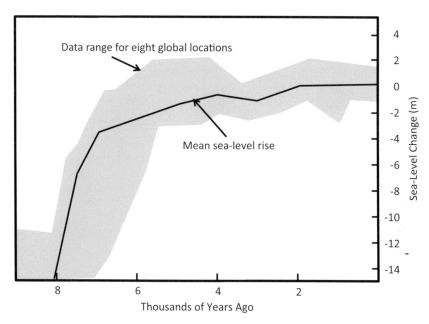

FIGURE 7.2 Global average sea-level curve showing how there was a steep rise in sea level after the end of the last ice age that slowed around 6,000–7,000 years ago (after Fleming et al. 1998 and Robert Rohde's climate change art compilation)

and pockets of low ground in which water collects, forming marshy areas within the floodplain. The islands and bars of the river are constantly shifting as material is eroded and then deposited. During meandering (B), the river is contained within a single migrating channel. Bars form on the inside of bends, which migrate outwards and downstream in a similar manner to the Nile in Upper Egypt that we discussed in Chapter 6. As meandering develops, crevasse deposits become rare and the floodplain is better drained, with fewer marshy pockets.

As a result of this process, the number of distributary channels began to decrease and the network of channels became less well connected (Stanley and Warne 1993). This meant that the delta changed towards the modern geometry, with distributaries reducing in number and radiating from a single point in the general area of Cairo, often known as the 'delta head'. Figure 7.4 shows how the initially rich network of habitats and channels of the LSC supported a large number of small communities, each of which could travel more or less directly from any one to any other. As meandering replaced the LSC, gradually propagating north, food resources became sparse in the interior of the delta and the interconnectivity of the channel network was

Large-scale crevassing

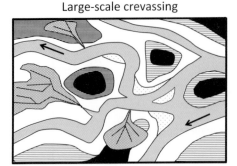

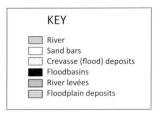

KEY

- River
- Sand bars
- Crevasse (flood) deposits
- Floodbasins
- River levées
- Floodplain deposits

Meandering

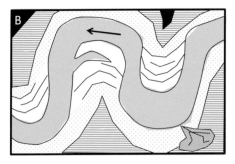

FIGURE 7.3 Diagram (after Pennington et al. 2016 and Weerts 1996) to show the environments encountered during (A) the large-scale crevassing stage of delta development, and (B) the meandering stage

reduced. At this time, settlements required resources from a larger area to survive and we see a hierarchy of settlements developing, with the capital at Memphis in a commanding position at the head of the delta.

Following a period of very high water and sediment levels during the Pleistocene, the sea level fell during the past ice age and the Nile cut down through the soft sediments of the Nile Valley and Delta leaving uplands of sand between the deeply cut channels. These are known as 'turtle-backs' or 'gezirehs' (Embabi 2004). As the sea level rose again in the Early Holocene (after 10,500 years), the water rose around the turtle-backs and a veneer of a few metres of dark-red sediment was deposited between the sands (Embabi 2004), leaving yellow sandy swales between the dark sediments of the flood channels (Bunbury et al. 2014). The turtle-backs were the ideal area for retreat during the annual flood (Tristant 2004) and communities grew up around their margins where there was access to the channels at low water and a ready retreat to the higher ground during times of flood. Floodplain rise

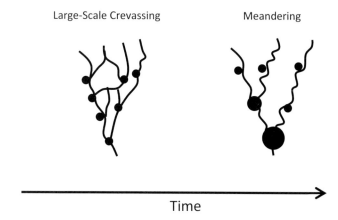

Large-Scale Crevassing   Meandering

Time

FIGURE 7.4 Diagram (after Pennington et al. 2016) to show how the LSC, predominant before 2000 BC, fostered abundant, well-fed and well-connected settlements, while the transition to meandering channels after 2000 BC favoured the development of larger settlements at the nodes of the delta distributary system

around these early settlements meant that they have been either drowned by Nile sediment or overbuilt by subsequent settlements that also sought the advantages of raised ground in a land imperilled by floodwaters.

It is this inundation of Nile waters that makes the geology and archaeology of this area so challenging and exciting. Tristant (2004) demonstrates that this history means that the Pre-Dynastic occupation of the delta can be little known. Examples that are known, such as the Pre-Dynastic part of the town of Buto, have been encountered at depth as the final stage of excavation of later sites that rise above the delta sediments. Known Pre-Dynastic sites are often below the current water table in areas where the later accumulations of settlement have been removed, for example at Sais where Penny Wilson used de-watering equipment to reach the remains of Pre-Dynastic settlements beneath the site of Sais at Sa El-Hagar (Wilson 2006) and at Kom el-Khilgan (Buchet and Midant-Reynes 2007). Other sites such as Naukratis cannot be further excavated to determine whether there is a core of earlier settlement due to the high groundwater levels. Buto's privileged location at the edge of a morass meant that it retained a supply of fresh water and avoided the *barari*, barren lands that are subject to saltwater conditions in winter and freshwater conditions in summer.

The better-known contemporaries of these turtle-back sites are those that flanked the delta on higher ground, for example Merimde Beni Salama (see Chapter 2) where evidence for high biodiversity in the adjacent swampy habitat is provided by the hippo–tibia steps (steps made out of hippo leg bones) of houses in the settlement (Eiwanger 1992). Micro-predators in the form of parasites and other pathogens were no doubt also abundant in the marshy areas (Groube 1996) – living in this area was a case of eat and be eaten.

Sedimentation through the mouths of the Nile generated delta lobes of their own, such as the one where the Damietta branch debouches into the sea. Longshore drift where the prevailing currents sweep sediment eastwards around the Mediterranean created sandbars along the coastline. The bars blocked the mouths of the embayments between the mouths of the Nile and created lagoons of which Lake Maryut, Lake Idku, Lake Borollos and Lake Manzala persist today (Stanley and Warne 1994). The lakes provided an important access to port cities like Tinnis during the rougher weather of the sailing season (Cooper 2014) which coincided with the period of the flood that rendered the lagoons fresh. Access to the lagoons was through cuts in the beach bar, many of which were fortified (e.g. the gate of Tinnis) (see Chapter 10).

The works of Stanley and Warne (1994) and Krom and Stanley (2003) provide our best insight into the subsurface structure of the delta. The latter investigation included some 140 boreholes around the margin of the delta, in which they could see evidence for the former mouths of the Nile channel and the effects of marine incursion into the coastal areas. Drill coring at Merimde Beni Salama (Rowland et al. 2014) showed that there is red mud typical of a body of Nile-supplied still water at around 4 m below the modern delta surface. The Neolithic activity at the site is located on the promontory created by the Wadi Gamal adjacent to this lake, and we conclude that this site was at the margins of a large swamp, probably the home of the hippopotami who provided the bones for the doorsteps and backed by a slightly greener 'desert' than today.

The locations of Pre-Dynastic sites are likely to have been dictated by the availability of fresh water throughout the year. At some coastal settlements, like Alexandria, fossil water stored in the ancient beach ridges provided some degree of water security, while at Merimde Beni Salama local pools were likely to have been freshwater and replenished by rains flowing down the Wadi Gamal. In the interior of the delta, the high Nile of the flood season ensured a summer freshwater supply, but during the winter the lowered Nile allowed saltwater incursion. By Roman and mediaeval times, the site of Tinnis was storing fresh water available in the summer in cisterns for use during the winter (Gascoigne 2007). In the more extreme case of Al-Farama (earlier Pelusium), water was supplied by boat from further inland; in this case the extra effort was warranted because the town was a staging post on the well-trodden route to the Levant. For these reasons, large ports were forced to lie inland to ensure a supply of fresh water, and the work of Stuart Borsch (Borsch 2000) suggests that in the Islamic period, if not earlier, a type of weir was in use, possibly to retain fresh water during times of low Nile and to prevent saltwater incursion.

With time, as seen in the Rhine Delta, there was a reduction in the number of mouths of the Nile. Ancient authors such as Herodotus and Strabo corroborate the presence of additional distributary channels. Earlier in this chapter we discussed the movement of the delta coast as Nile waters rose then fell in response to melting ice sheets and sedimentation. Stanley and Warne (1994) also revealed a return from saline to freshwater conditions as the delta coast moved seawards again. Inland from the coast, gharaghets, or natural saltpans, formed; these could also be accessed from the delta distributary system and were a source of highly prized salt for trade.

By the Old Kingdom, the outline of the delta was much as it is today, with the exception of the north-eastern part, now Lake Manzala, which was still part of the sea. For the rest, coastal lagoons were backed by large tracts of marsh. The delta site of Kom el-Hisn was studied by Wenke (1988) who made a detailed examination of the faunal and floral remains. There is abundant evidence at Kom el-Hisn for use of cattle dung as fuel but there are few remains of cattle among the bones collected, which are principally of pigs, sheep and goats. In addition, the fish bones are mainly bodies, with few heads found, leading to the conclusion that these were decapitated, preserved fish imported to the site. A picture emerges of a ranch where cattle were reared in pens for export to the capital zone, while the herders ate other foods including imported fish. Wenke and his team concluded that in the Old Kingdom Kom el-Hisn was the site of a cattle ranch of the type that is depicted in the Tomb of Ti, with its scenes of cattle being delivered by men from the delta supplying the capital zone, as well as agricultural activity by delta men identifiable by their stiff reed kilts (Figure 7.5).

From the end of the Old Kingdom until the establishment of the New Kingdom the lagoons, marshes and salt pans of the delta fell under the control of feudal 'Asiatics' who had strong trading contacts with the Levant, and a mixture of Asiatics and Egyptians were settled at Avaris (Tel el-Daba; see Bourriau in Shaw 2000). In the eastern delta, Libyans made territorial gains in the marshes of the western delta.

The New Kingdom opened with military campaigns to the north and south that reunited the Egyptian empire under the pharaoh. By this time meandering channels dominated the environment of the Nile Valley and

FIGURE 7.5 Drawing after tomb relief of cattle herders arriving at the Old Kingdom Tomb of Ptahhotep at Saqqara, west of Memphis

Delta. Trade with the eastern Mediterranean became increasingly important and regulation (and taxation) of the various mouths of the Nile became of great interest. Memphis, strategically placed where the delta narrows down, was again renewed as the capital, and the enormous Temple of Ptah was laid out by Ramses II in boggy ground between the islands of the garden city of Memphis (Bunbury et al. 2017). John Cooper (2014) has shown that the central distributary of the Nile was a strategically poor place to enter the delta since it was vulnerable to strong winds and the rough water that occurs where the Mediterranean currents intersect those of the outflowing Nile.

In terms of the basic requirements for a thriving human community, these ancients would have been looking for sheltered areas (away from the elements); fresh water (with an abundance of wildlife); and a flat terrain allowing both easy access to trade routes (either by sea or road) and for the development of agricultural practices. The subsidiary mouths proved safer to access and thus important trading towns grew up on these branches, for example Naukratis on the Canopic branch. Work by Manfred Bietak suggests that the earliest ports were located around 30 km inland of the delta coast where marine influence disappeared and where a ready supply of fresh water became available (Bietak 2017). From a navigational perspective, the continued tectonic subsidence of the Manzala lagoon maintained maritime conditions in a sheltered location.

As the mouths of the Nile reduced in number so did the area of the marshes and the lagoons. In addition, the beach ridge of the north-eastern delta gradually migrated seawards until it approached its current position around two thousand years ago. Continued subsidence along the faults that border Lake Manzala to the east and west ensured that the lagoon only shrank slowly to its current size.

The process of management of the waterways of the delta has continued to the present day, with interventions that were begun by Nasser in the 1930s. Irrigation programmes designed to reclaim the low terraces that surround the edge of the delta have also extended the area of cultivation into an area that was formerly desert. The area of the delta is vulnerable to sea-level rise, and this is discussed further in Chapter 11.

8

RENEWED STRENGTH IN THE SOUTH: THE RISE OF THEBES (KARNAK) AND MANAGEMENT OF THE MINOR CHANNELS OF THE NILE

D URING THE MIDDLE KINGDOM, THEBES BEGAN TO GROW IN importance and temples in the area that is now known as Karnak were founded on sandbanks emerging from the Nile. The theme of architecture on islands is prominent in ancient Egypt and a number of important sites have a foundation myth that includes an island. By the New Kingdom, Nile management had reached new peaks and evidence from Karnak, the Faiyum and Memphis illustrate the scope of landscape projects that were envisioned by the state. Climate amelioration during the early New Kingdom ushered in a period of relative stability and prosperity, and the Egyptian empire reaching arguably its greatest extent, with connections to the south with Nubia and as far north as the Levant. The return of some rain to the deserts allowed old waterholes and routes to open up in the wadis around the Nile Valley, such as the area of the Theban Mountain and some more long-distance routes through Kharga and Dakhla.

The first king of the New Kingdom, Ahmose I, launched a campaign to regain control of the delta from the Hyksos and, when he succeeded, ushered in a reign administered from Thebes, towards the south of Egypt. The terri-tory of this realm extended south into Nubia with gold-mining operations in northern Sudan. To the north, absolute conquests into the Near East were supplemented with treaties with kings further northwards, as far as Hatti, the kingdom of the Hittites (Bryce 2005). Panels at Karnak Temple report the later 19th Dynasty victories against the Hittites at the battle of Kadesh Thebes, which testify, although perhaps in exaggerated form, to a wide range of conquests. Further evidence for powerful connections over-seas comes from the communities of expatriate workers that came to Egypt, for example linen workers at Akhmin in Middle Egypt or the horse breeders of Thebes who used a specially constructed area along the side of the Birket Habu, a large reservoir, for training imported horses. Expeditions to the

FIGURE 8.1 Myrrh roots still remaining at Deir el-Bahri on the West Bank at Thebes (Luxor)

south, to Punt (probably modern Ethiopia), during the time of Hatshepsut and depicted in her mortuary temple at Deir el-Bahri, brought back many valuable goods, including myrrh trees whose roots still survive at the temple (Figure 8.1). The milder temperatures probably ensured that the myrrh trees and other tropical species could be grown more easily during this period.

By the time of Amenhotep III, large amounts of gold were being won from Nubia (Spence et al. 2009) and used to sweeten relations with kings to the north, including the Mitanni, a people who had a kingdom that spanned modern-day south-east Turkey and the northern parts of Iran and Iraq (Moran 1992). The New Kingdom archive of cuneiform texts on clay tablets, the Amarna Letters, contains much correspondence from kingdoms to the north requesting gold among other riches. In Nubia, examination of the extensive mining around the Temple of Sesebi (Spence et al. 2009) suggests that conditions in the area were wetter at that time than they are now. There is also some indication, from mining activity in the wadis to the north of the temple, that there was at least seasonal rainfall that could be used in the extraction of the gold by riffling over the natural schist rocks.

Rodrigues (2000) studied freshwater mussel shells in the nearby Wadi Howar that indicate much wetter conditions there than further to the north, where sites such as Giza had already been enclosed by drifting desert sands (Bunbury et al. 2009). Similarly, Gebel al-Asr, a little to the north, was not encapsulated by blown sand until after the Middle Kingdom use of the mines and buildings around Quartz Ridge (Shaw et al. 2001). To the east, in the Dongola Reach of the Nile, over 450 sites were found together with clear evidence for palaeo-channels of the Nile, the banks of which were densely settled during the Kerma period (c. 2500–1500 BC). The demise of these palaeo-channels resulted in a dramatic fall in the population of the region by the first millennium BC (Welsby 2013).

By the New Kingdom, techniques in the management of both islands and channels are evident, including the use of the minor channels near islands as harbours and the laying out of new temples within strategically blocked old channels. Chains of islands are common in the bends of the Nile channel, where sediment that has been eroded from elsewhere is redeposited. Generally, sandbars and islands form close to the bends where the channel profile is asymmetric and the water flows faster and therefore erodes the outside of the bend. As the river enters the straight on the way to the next bend, the channel broadens and becomes symmetric in profile. This point is known as the 'ferry point' since it is where it is easiest to cross the river by ferry. Towards the next bend the channel starts to become asymmetric again and sand is deposited as bars on the inside of the bend. This pattern continues through the length of the river.

Even if a river channel is initially straight, small disturbances in the channel will grow until the river forms a meandering pattern. In microcosm, the meandering Californian stream in Figure 8.2 demonstrates these processes at work. The upstream, background bend has a steep erosional bank to the

FIGURE 8.2 Californian stream that demonstrates the process of meandering

left on the outside of the bend, with a series of point bars to the right on the inside of the bend. As the river meanders into the foreground the water in the channel crosses the river bed to the outside of the bend to the right, which is the erosional bank, while point bars form to the left on the inside of the bend.

In many cases (e.g. Mississippi, USA) bends continue to exaggerate until alternate bends meet and a loop is cut off to form an oxbow lake. In Egypt the sinuosity of the river is limited by the relatively difficult to erode margins of the Nile Canyon (see also Chapter 3, Dufton 2008 and Stølum 1997) and so meander cut-offs are rare. The effect is that bends appear to migrate outwards and downstream until they are 'turned' by the walls of the Nile Canyon. In some places, like Middle Egypt, where the floodplain is wide it may take many thousands of years for the river to cross the floodplain, but in others like Armant (Figure 6.3), the floodplain is restricted in width and the river is effectively limited to one of two possible channels divided by an island. Where island formation and capture is added to the normal migration of the stream, migration rates of up to 9 km/millennium may be reached, considerably above the normal mean of 2 km/millennium (Bunbury et al. 2009).

FIGURE 8.3 Aerial photograph of the river bend north of Karnak looking north,
showing how the Nile floodplain impinges upon the desert (top left)

Small sandbars accrete and consolidate with time, eventually emerging
as islands through processes that were studied by Duckworth (2009). The
sediments associated with the growth and expansion of such islands as those
in Figure 8.3 are known from an auger study at Al-Zaniyah island 2 km
north of Karnak in Luxor (see Appendix). This pattern of sedimentation
is common across Egypt and is associated with the formation of the early
parts of the site at Karnak as well as at Memphis. The island habitat has a
number of advantages. It has easy access to river transport and fresh water,
it has freshly deposited rich soils and it is relatively safe from erosion since
the channels on either side can transfer water from one to the other without
eroding the island. These advantages were evident to ancient inhabitants of
the Nile Valley as much as to the modern inhabitants.

Excavations at Luxor Old Garden Site by the SCA dig school show that,
as the island there accreted and changed, there were adaptations to the way in
which the island was occupied. However, the lifespan of an island was probably less than a century, since the minor channel tends to become blocked at
one end, leaving it stagnant and starved of sediment. Subsequent inundations
gradually fill the channel until it becomes a marsh and eventually fills in.

FIGURE 8.4 The still backwaters of the Nile, rich with biodiversity. There is abundant weed, habitat for fish in the shallows, which provides food for waterfowl that live in the reed beds. The palm trees indicate the agricultural Nile floodplain beyond the reed beds (photo Rose Collis)

Taryn Duckworth's work (2009) helps to illustrate the ways in which islands can be used and why they were so important in ancient Egypt. Islands, being in the middle of the Nile channel, were easily accessible to river traffic and provided fresh water. The channel on one side was generally fast-flowing while the other, minor channel, was a backwater. These backwaters remain a rich habitat today with reed beds, fish and birdlife (Figure 8.4).

Angus Graham has studied sandbars in detail and finds that, in the Nile, they are generally horned bars. Initially, a sandbank forms and, as the current is decelerated to either side of the sandbank, more sand is deposited to form a horseshoe-shaped island. At the upstream end, there is solid ground suitable for a few fields or perhaps a farm building, while inside the horseshoe is a swampy area where fish spawn and rich silt is deposited. Agriculture on the island is supported by the fertility of the fresh sediment and the ready access to fresh water. Figure 8.5, based on studies of the islands of Luxor, shows how agricultural activity and other uses lead to the development and stabilisation of new islands.

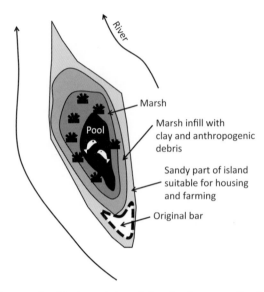

FIGURE 8.5 Diagram after Duckworth (2009) showing how a sandbank evolves into a horned bar, then an island and, around a century later, becomes bonded to the riverbank.

In the Luxor reach today, fishermen use light skiffs to explore the inner horseshoe, while herdsmen force cattle through the water (Duckworth 2009) to graze on the fresh plants on the island and stir and enhance the sediment with their hooves and their dung. Reeds and other plants that arrive with the cattle baffle further sediment, increasing the stability of the sandbar until it grows large enough for more substantial buildings and more extensive crop planting during the low season of the Nile. In the days of the flood, additional silt deposited during the inundation prepared the ground for a new crop. A sequence of thin silts at Karnak, which were separated by burnt layers, may be indicative of just such a use of the original Karnak island (Bunbury, Graham and Hunter 2008). Alongside the island the minor channel was an ideal location for the domestic activity, landing boats, brewing, baking and no doubt laundering that we know took place at the river's edge, menaced by crocodiles ('The washerman washes on the shore with the crocodile as his neighbour', from 'Satire of the Trades, tr. Lichtheim 1973).

The area around the son et lumière at Karnak, sometimes described as Tell Karnak, appears to show a river levee with steps down to the water, very similar to the stone steps that serve the riverbank in modern times (Millett and Masson 2011). Alongside any island with its attendant domestic activity, the minor channel, although it may be deep, has slow water and is a suitable habitat for large fish. Seining (fishing using nets) for large fish still takes place in these minor channels in the Edfu area, and the prevalence of these in the remains from the temple at Nekhen/Hierakonpolis (Van Neer et al. 2002, Van Neer and Linseele 2009; see also Chapter 3) seems to indicate that the practice has persisted since the Old Kingdom, when a channel flanked the site. With these combined resources, access to fresh water, transport and a variety of foodstuffs, islands seem to have been idealised; many appear in tomb scenes of the rivers of the afterlife, particularly in the scenes from the 19th Dynasty of the New Kingdom. Heaven was indeed an island in the Nile.

Evidence from other archaeological island sites suggests that there was a sophisticated set of strategies involved in managing islands, including groins composed of pots of rubble at Karnak (Ted Brock, personal communication), retaining walls at the Luxor Old Garden Site (AERA excavation visit) and the use of low-lying areas for industrial processes, for example brick clamps, during the dry season resulting in a scatter of slag and other waste materials left behind. Other examples of island foundation myths and topography include Hermopolis (see Chapter 5).

Excavations at Karnak suggest that the points where boats landed at the temples were celebrated at barque shrines, although the shrines became more distant from the water as the channels migrated away and, in the examples at Karnak, were then incorporated into the temple structure while new barque shrines were added to the waterfront. For example, the barque shrine of Seti I was subsequently incorporated into the court of the first pylon at Karnak (see also Chapter 6). No doubt the opportunity for new display provided by the freshly accreting land was relished by the extant ruler since the new waterfront could then be occupied by their monuments. Similarly, waterfront structures such as slipways were modified to bring them back to the contemporary waterfront. Dufton in his work on the koms of the Abydos area postulated that towns had 'rolled' as the river moved. The old town, further from the water as the river migrated, was superseded by new developments along the waterfront, and as migration continued yet more new developments were made. The old town by this time was falling into disrepair and in similar examples at Naslet es-Saman (near Giza) and at Memphis the ruined town then became a quarry for stone for the new construction zone. The product of this rolling is a raised area of the floodplain (with few standing monuments) over which the town has passed.

New Kingdom Memphis provides us with an example of an ambitious project to segment a waning channel. By building dykes, Pédro Gonçalves (Cambridge University PhD dissertation in preparation) shows us that low ground left by a waning channel could be used to provide a new temple site for the Ptah Temple. The remains of the channel served as harbours to the north and south. Much of the early evidence was then muted by an even more ambitious Saite scheme in the seventh century BC to develop a large mound at Kom Tuman as the seat of the palace of Apries (Gunn 1927). However, sufficient evidence of the earlier New Kingdom project remains to reconstruct the landscape intervention.

Pédro Gonçalves (Cambridge University PhD thesis in preparation) in his work analysing the Survey of Memphis cores has reconstructed the development of this site. He shows how the early settlement at Memphis was founded around the shores of an island in the Old Kingdom and developed further during the Middle Kingdom. In his history, Manetho attributes the founding of Memphis to Menes, one of the earliest kings of the united Egypt. Gonçalves posits that, at times of low Niles, the settlement expanded towards the river, but that at times of high Niles it was eroded and forced to retreat. With time, and during the Middle Kingdom, marshy areas became gradually infilled by anthropogenic activity but, by the New Kingdom, more ambitious landscape management schemes were being planned. These included segmenting the waning channels of the valley to produce an area of land between two harbours. The Temple of Ptah at Memphis was constructed between these two harbours on reclaimed land. The main Nile continued to migrate towards the east as a series of islands formed and were captured. In common with Karnak, the site continued to develop in the waterfront area, while older parts of the city were abandoned and quarried for stone and landfill material.

Memphite monuments explored by the Survey of Memphis and AERA are shown in Figure 8.6, with the inferred positions of ancient waterways as described by Pédro Gonçalves in his interpretation of some 150 exploratory cores from the area. Evidence from fine-grained mud and contemporary New Kingdom sediments at the same level show that the waning channel was dissected by east–west embankments and the temple laid out on the new low ground. The North Birka (N) and the South Birka (S) remained wet and may have been used as harbours. The map (Figure 8.6) shows the main ruins of Memphis around the modern village of Mit Rahina. The site is so complex and extensive that the mounds are divided into a number of smaller eminences (koms) whose names are shown here. The pale shading shows channels extant during the early Middle Kingdom development of the city in the areas around Kom Rabi and Kom Fakhry, while the dark shading shows the formalised waterways of the New Kingdom. Much of western Memphis was later cut down to build the eminence of Kom Tuman

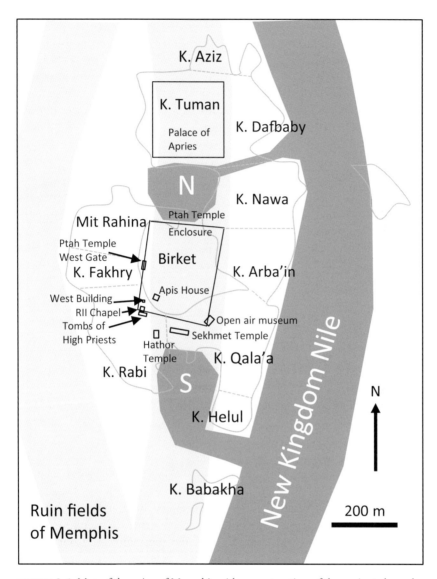

FIGURE 8.6 Map of the ruins of Memphis with reconstruction of the ancient channels

by the Saite pharaohs. Not long after these developments, Memphis fell into disuse and was replaced by other sites in the Babylon (Old Cairo) area (see capital zone in Chapter 10).

Evidence that Nile management was not only reaching new levels at this time but that climate amelioration was reopening the desert to travellers

FIGURE 8.7 'Stairway' in the Theban mountain; the floor of a natural crack has been smoothed to allow safe passage up the cliff that is c. 30 m high

comes from the Theban Mountain, a block of up-faulted limestones, close to Luxor. New arrivals in Egypt are often struck by the sharp boundary between the green of the cultivation and the sandy yellows of the desert. The Theban Mountain in the Luxor area is no exception, and today the massif forms a largely barren area, a refuge for jackals and gerbils with almost

FIGURE 8.8 Palimpsest columns at the New Kingdom Temple of Sesebi in northern Sudan

no groundwater and little vegetation. However, in the New Kingdom the area became a very busy necropolis with valleys devoted to the burial of kings, queens and nobles, including the Valley of the Kings. We know that water was not very abundant in the area since the workmen of the valley were forced to live in the settlement of Deir el-Medina at the edge of the floodplain. Here they had no access to water themselves and were dependent upon water carriers to supply them as well as sending out the laundry to be washed at the Nile, as we learn from the numerous ostraca that were thrown into an enormous pit at the settlement (McDowell 1999). Indeed, the excavation of the 'Great Pit' may have been an ultimately unsuccessful effort to dig a well deep enough to reach the groundwater and its use as a giant rubbish tip was a secondary purpose.

However, other evidence suggests that at least during the latter part of the 18th Dynasty rainfall may have arrived in the desert accompanied by additional human activity. One example is the use of tombs in Wadi Bairiya on the route from the palace at Malqata, which were excavated by Piers Litherland (2015). His team showed that, at the time of preparation of the tombs during the 18th Dynasty reign of Amenhotep III, wet mud lay around

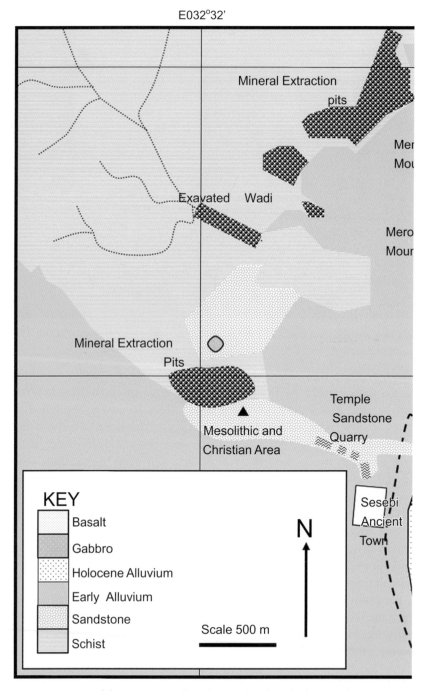

E032°32'

Mineral Extraction

pits

Mer
Mou

Exavated   Wadi

Mero
Mour

Mineral Extraction

Pits

Temple

Sandstone

Quarry

Mesolithic and

Christian Area

KEY

Basalt

Gabbro

Holocene Alluvium

Early Alluvium

Sandstone

Schist

N

Scale 500 m

Sesebi
Ancient
Town

FIGURE 8.9 Map of the area surrounding the Temple of Sesebi showing the areas of mining activity widely distributed around the site of the temple and town

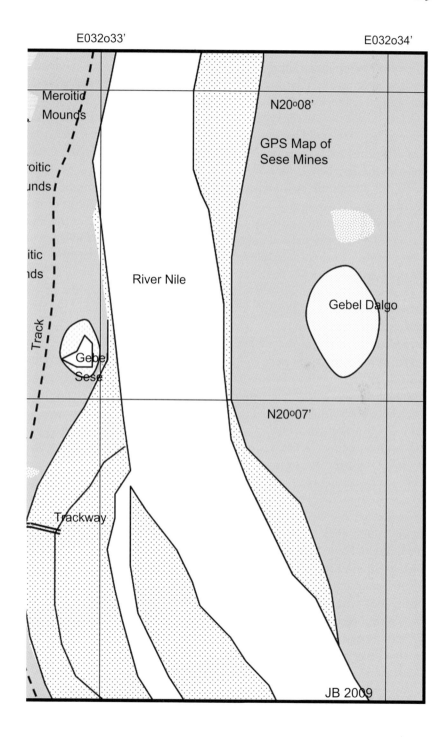

E032o33' E032o34'

Meroitic
Mounds

N20o08'

GPS Map of
Sese Mines

oitic
unds

itic
ds

River Nile

Gebel Dalgo

Track

Gebel
Sese

N20o07'

Trackway

JB 2009

the site and took impressions of footprints and plaster-making along with samples of New Kingdom pottery. Subsequent visitors, in particular state-sponsored parties of the Third Intermediate Period, re-excavated the tombs not long after but, by that time, the dried mud had been covered by other rain-washed sediment, preserving it.

A little further east in the Valley of the Kings, the tomb of Tutankhamun, a minor king of the 18th Dynasty, was concealed not long after its completion by a debris flow occasioned by torrential rain in the valley (Stephen Cross, report to the Supreme Council of Antiquities). A little later, other evidence for rainfall during the 19th Dynasty comes from inscriptions on the rocks describing visits to waterfalls that poured off the limestone plateau of the high desert (Dorn 2016). Activity along paths in the Theban Mountain also burgeoned during this period, with numerous cairns, trackways and heaps of pottery refuse crossing the desert from Luxor in the direction of Farshout, and the existence of active wells the north.

The 'stairway' in Figure 8.7 is a testament to the traffic along the desert paths. A natural crack in the rock was filled so that pedestrians and possibly donkeys could ascend an incline through the passage. In the 18th Dynasty in particular, activity in the wadis spread further and further to the west and there is evidence for wells and huts scattered through the desert. One particularly large mound of pottery debris, possibly associated with a spring in a natural cave, reveals the extent to which rain has fallen since these times. Sherds accumulated near the cave from the New Kingdom onwards and during subsequent rainfall were washed downstream through the wadi system for more than 8 km. That the sherds are rounded demonstrates that they were brought by streams rushing down the wadis rather than being deposited by passing travellers.

Further south at Sesebi, a New Kingdom colonial town near the Nile in the region of the Second Cataract in northern Sudan, a period of wetter climate is also evident. The site itself is an enclosure (Spence et al. 2009) containing a New Kingdom temple initially constructed from the local sandstone during the reign of Amenhotep IV (later Akhenaten). The town persisted until the time of Ramses II. The columns are palimpsest columns (Figure 8.8) with parts of each of two generations of inscriptions visible. They were originally decorated by Akhenaten, but were later replastered and redecorated by Seti I. After the plaster had been eroded away all that remained was the lower relief of the early inscription punctured by the deeper parts of the later one.

The enclosed town of Sesebi is relatively small but in the massifs and wadis around the site are many square kilometres of pitting, the result of excavation for alluvial gold (Figure 8.9). The ore, much in the manner of the Hammamat mines in the Eastern Desert of Egypt, was collected from the gold-bearing lodes and transported back to the temple site where it could be ground up on the numerous indurated schist grindstones that litter the site of Sesebi. The ore was enriched under the secure conditions of the temple before export northwards into Egypt, where it would be distributed from temples like Karnak. Contemporary correspondence from the Amarna Letters indicates that the gold dust was also a valued export further north (Moran 1992). Seasonally, local rainfall seems also to have been used to separate the gold from the ore by riffling over the naturally rough surface of the schist bedrock. Whilst communications with Egypt were strong, it seems likely that the additional rainfall in the area made it possible to sustain the colony and extract the gold without heavy reliance upon supplies from the homeland.

By the New Kingdom, there seems to have been a good understanding on the part of the inhabitants of the Nile Valley of how the river and its islands behaved. This working knowledge allowed them to exert a degree of control over the mighty Nile waters, turning what might have been environmental disorder and chaos into meaningful and advantageous habitats, capable of sustaining not only life but livelihoods. The scene was set for even larger and more elaborate river management schemes from the New Kingdom onwards.

9

HIGH TIDES OF EMPIRE: THE
NEW KINGDOM TO THE
ROMAN PERIOD – DEVELOPMENT
OF LARGE-SCALE NILE
WATER MANAGEMENT

ARGUABLY PERIODS OF HIGH GLOBAL TEMPERATURE PROMOTED the expansion of successful empires, by expanding the Nile floodplain and greening the deserts and their wadi systems. The New Kingdom and the Roman periods, both times of high global temperature, were also times when empires expanded to their maximum extent. They are therefore understandably the periods in which water management schemes were at their most ambitious.

We already know from the Gurob Harem Palace Project (see gurob.org. uk for details) that by the time of Thutmose III in the early New Kingdom the king could arrange large landscape-scale projects such as the provision of water to some 100 km² of the Faiyum basin through a regulator at Gurob. The Gurob Harem Palace was constructed on the desert edge just to the south of the entrance to the Faiyum Oasis (Figure 9.1). From the Neolithic to the Old Kingdom (4000–2200 BC) a lake filled the Faiyum basin, reaching almost to the 20 m contour. The extent of the much-reduced modern Lake Qarun is shown with dark shading. This oasis was naturally refreshed during the annual flood as water poured through a spillway that led from the Nile. After the end of the Old Kingdom, however, the lake started a punctuated process of drying down to form the rather briny residual lake of Lake Qarun that remains today. Its surface is currently 47 m below sea level and has caused deep scouring of the earlier lake sediments. From the Middle Kingdom, schemes, particularly that of Amnemhat III, were conceived to regreen the oasis. These were succeeded by the New Kingdom project to create a precursor of the Hawara Canal overseen by the palace at Gurob. Boreholes reveal that water was diverted (Figure 9.2) from the Bahr Yusuf at A in Figure 9.1 into the depression restoring the lake to the 17 m contour

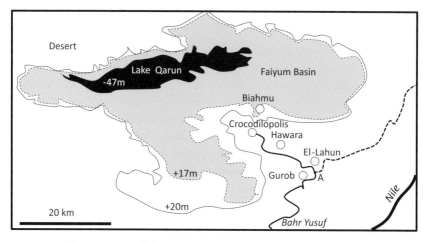

FIGURE 9.1 Contour map of the Faiyum Basin (after Gasperini 2010)

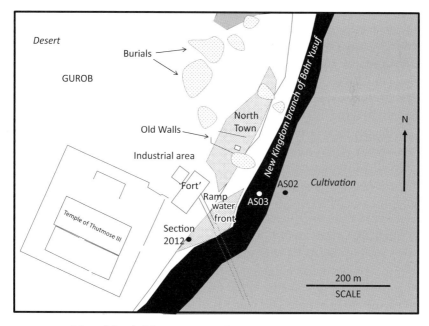

FIGURE 9.2 Map of Gurob (after Brunton and Engelbach 1927) incorporating the work of the Gurob Harem Palace Project (unpublished SCA reports)

(grey shaded area) and commemorated by the construction of colossi at Biahmu.

Recent work with Ian Shaw at the Gurob Harem Palace Project and including a range of cores drilled by Ellie Hughes shows that there was a New Kingdom channel that was dug along the base of the desert scarp, rounded the corner at Lahun and fed into the oasis. No doubt the mud excavated from the channel was a useful contribution to the construction of an impressive palace from which the water could be controlled. Earlier excavators including Petrie and Brunton and Engelbach (1927) described a strong building that they tentatively identified as a 'fort'. The fort, which is surrounded by an industrial area from which kilns have been excavated by Anna Hodgkinson (Shaw 2010), may be more of an administrative centre than a defensive structure. A ramp leads from the fort down to a landing area (Figure 9.2).

Satellite image analysis by Sarah Parcak showed that there were other possible buildings to the north of the fort (North Town). Today, erosion has flattened the topography of the site and only a thin veneer from the base of the mud-brick walls remains of these northern constructions, but the prevalence of 'lady-on-a-bed' clay impressions, perhaps votive, which have been catalogued by Jan Picton, suggests that the inhabitants shared the normal domestic concerns of the period. Recent excavations by Anna Kathrin Hodgkinson and Dan Boatwright (2009 and 2010) in the area near magnetic anomalies show that there are kilns and other industrial activity near to the fort (Figure 9.3), further strengthening the impression of a burgeoning elite community at the palace. Although the site today has an aspect of almost unparalleled bleakness, our reconstructions suggest that at different times the settlement was composed of the palace and the fort (Marine Yoyotte, personal communication). The town continued to develop during the 19th Dynasty of the New Kingdom and also into the Ptolemaic period.

Similarly, further south in Thebes (Luxor) we see landscape design in the work of Amenhotep III who, from the Theban Landscape and Waterscapes Project (Graham et al. 2015), seems to have brought a channel to his reservoir of Birket Habu alongside the palace at Malqata to continue in front of his memorial temple. The Birket has an area of around 2 km² and lies at the western edge of the floodplain. The basin required the excavation of a large amount of sediment and may have been an extension of an earlier natural basin (Aude Grazer-Ohara 2012). Unfortunately, its original purpose is obscure although the scale of this and some other similar earthworks to the east, of less certain age, is indisputable. It is notable, however, that the basin of Birket Habu captures two of the streams that flow from the wadis into the

FIGURE 9.3 Excavation of kilns in the area of the 'fort' by Anna Kathrin Hodgkinson (Hodgkinson and Boatright 2009 and 2010)

Nile Valley at this point, indicating that they were likely to have been active at that time.

An additional birket to the east may have had a similar channel to attach it to the Nile and the provision of quays at the temples of Medamud and Tod suggests that they also were provided with access channels. These projects demonstrate a clear understanding of how mud excavated from supply channels could be used to provide embankments or mud brick for palaces as part of a civil engineering project. Or similarly how, with the excavation of Birket Habu, a raised area could be created to house the settlement and to provide an artificial plateau and mounds. These elevations were suitable for horse-training and viewing equestrian contests as well as festival flotillas on the lake.

The subsequent attempt by Akhenaten to establish a completely new city at Amarna, apparently divorced from the Nile, may have reflected excessive ambition on the part of Akhenaten, or equally an unexpected change back to dryer conditions or migration of the river that rendered the site unworkable soon after it was constructed. During the Ramesside (19th Dynasty of the New Kingdom) period and after the return to Thebes, many of these earlier 18th Dynasty schemes were taken up and renewed.

Ambitious projects during the Ptolemaic period include a link from the Pelusiac branch of the Nile excavated towards the Red Sea, later re-excavated after the Roman annexation of Egypt, to join the Nile and the eastern Mediterranean to the Red Sea via the Bitter Lakes. The next peak of global temperature dates to the Roman period, which began in Egypt in 30 AD. The grain-producing potential of Egypt was exploited as it had been earlier during the New Kingdom. Grain harvests were taxed and during the flood season large grain barges travelled northwards, accumulating grain to supply Alexandria as well as the capital of the Roman Empire. Luxury products from the region included wine which was said to be of high quality.

Whether it was political strength at home, a milder climate in the desert or a combination of both factors, the New Kingdom was also a time of increased mining activity in the deserts. Interest in the Wadi Hammamat gold mines as well as exploitation of emeralds and many other mineral resources of the desert meant the creation of cross-desert routes. There were expeditions far afield down the Red Sea, like the expedition to Punt mounted by Hatshepsut, or up the Nile to the gold mining in the area of the Second Cataract (modern North Sudan). Colonies were established to manage these enterprises, for example Sesebi in the Nubian Gold Fields (Spence et al. 2009; see Chapter 8). Cross-desert routes with fortlets and guard towers were constructed in the Eastern Desert and in the Saharan oases, providing safe access for official functionaries and produce. Evidence for wells that were first used in the New Kingdom and revived in the Roman period suggests that greater rainfall in the deserts at this time created groundwater reserves that could be used by desert travellers. The Eastern Desert also saw the produc-tion of quarry stone on an unprecedented scale, including Mons Porphyrites and Mons Claudianus, both in the Eastern Desert, which produced imperial porphyry and a gold-flecked granite, respectively. A large octagonal Roman well, Bir umm-Fawakir in the Wadi Hammamat, was excavated to support the gold mines and remains in use today.

In the cases of both the New Kingdom and the Roman period, the cli-mate excursions were short-lived. The Lament to Amun, found on a New Kingdom papyrus c. 1200 BC, may reflect the negative side of these changes.

> ... protect me in this year of bitter confrontation. God shines in the sun; yet he will not shine, winter crowds hard upon summer. [... spoken ...] ... by horned beasts on our burning deserts.
>
>   Lament to Amun, tr. John L. Foster (2001)

While the main channel of the Nile remained difficult to manage, the minor channels could now be controlled and having less water and lower velocities

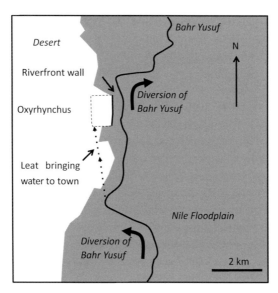

FIGURE 9.4 Reconstruction of the water management that supplied the town of Oxyrhynchus

meandered on a much smaller scale than the main river. During Ptolemaic and Roman times this manageability was developed and exploited. The Bahr Yusuf, the minor western branch of the Nile, was an ideal partner to the development of a town and, from the example of Oxyrhynchus, a sophisticated pattern of location within the landscape and symbiosis with it emerges. As we have seen from the New Kingdom examples of Karnak and Memphis, sites in the Nile Valley were vulnerable to alienation from the Nile channel during migration. From Ptolemaic times a new approach was developed. The solution was to build in the desert and bring the river to the site. These techniques, first developed on the more manageable Bahr Yusuf, were eventually developed during Roman times to include the main Nile (see also Hermopolis in Chapter 5).

At Oxyrhynchus (Subias et al. 2013), the Bahr Yusuf was diverted to the desert edge where the town was founded (Figure 9.4). Physical remains of the Roman town are visible but more exceptionally its enormous archive of rubbish dumped in the desert also survived. From these documents, we learn of lovers' tiffs, a kind gift of a puppy to a lonely bride now far from home and many more mundane matters pertinent to the running of the town (Parsons 2007). The combined record of the archaeology and the documents shows that a leat (channel), taken from the Bahr Yusuf upstream where it joined the desert edge, brought water to a large tank at the upper, desert edge of the town. From here, a grid of channels served the town in all but the lowest part of the river's annual cycle. The channels brought fresh water into the houses and delivered the used water to the river below the town, where there was a waterfront wall. At times when the water was exhausted, a man was employed to raise water to the town and we learn from his correspondence that in a particularly long dry season he felt disgruntled. A downstream embankment probably also provided a nutrient-rich marsh.

In Middle Egypt, where the floodplain is wide enough to have preserved traces of much past activity, a strategy emerged of digging cross ditches between sets of levees associated with abandoned channels and minor channels like the Bahr Yusuf (Subias et al. 2013). Most of these abandoned channels flow broadly north–south so relatively short cross-links between them could be dug to bring water to new areas or to turn an abandoned channel into a reservoir. Arguably, it was the Romans who had finally attained mastery of the Nile.

In addition to their hydro-engineering of the Nile, the Romans also hydro-engineered the desert expanding lines of manawir (qanats), chains of linked wells, a technology first introduced by the Persians (Figure 9.5). New settlements in the desert sprang up around the old playa basins where lines of manawir several kilometres long could tap sufficient water from the local surface water sandstone (SWS) to irrigate the fertile silts of the old lake beds. Examples of these include Um el Dabadeb and Ain Manawir in the Kharga Basin. A manawir was constructed by digging multiple vertical shafts to a gently sloping tunnel. The narrow tunnels of the qanat were accessible for maintenance either along the tunnel or through the shafts, which were often supplied with footholds. The fill excavated from the underground network of tunnels was deposited around the mouth of the shafts and can be seen on the land surface above. Parts of this system have been excavated to reveal the subsurface structure.

Other ingenious technological solutions for gleaning water from the desert include 'jar-wells' (Figure 9.6) of a type seen at a Coptic hermitage at Ain Amur and in Roman and Coptic settlements of the Theban Mountain. At these sites, large jars or amphorae were placed under an overhang, enhanced by excavation, in a stream bed. One such site on the Theban Mountain had a group of fourteen huts apparently supported by a dozen or so water-collection points of this type. Even a modest trickle into each jar from the limestone aquifer could supply day-to-day needs and the remains suggest that deeper wells were also used when required.

To the north in the delta, the defensive capabilities of the waterways were exploited at sites like Kom Firin (Figure 9.7). The site, in the west of the delta

FIGURE 9.5 Roman qanat system at Ain Lebakh in the Kharga Oasis, still in use

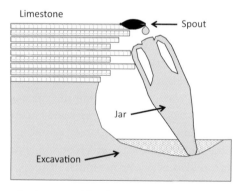

FIGURE 9.6 A jar-well where a trickle of water can be harvested by the emplacement of a jar in the stream bed

along a now-extinct branch of the delta distributary system, was long-lived. It formed part of a chain of sites located on mounds that flank an ancient waterway close to the modern Firiniya Canal (Spencer 2014). Delta towns were frequently menaced by marauders from the west and Kom Firin's location on an island surrounded by channels made it a good defensive position.

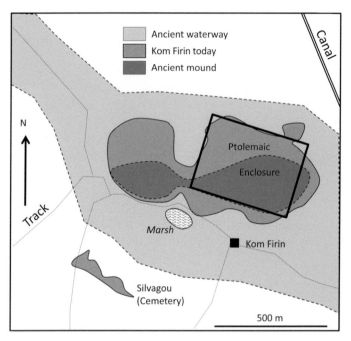

FIGURE 9.7 Map of Kom Firin showing the area of auger coring used in the landscape interpretation. Small squares indicate the settlements of Kom Firin and Silvagou, while the large rectangle indicates the extent of the Ptolemaic Temple

The core of the site was a relict Pleistocene gezireh at the western end of which a settlement mound (kom) accumulated. Burials from the Middle Kingdom and Second Intermediate Period nearby suggest that there was earlier settlement but the town burgeoned during the 19th Dynasty of the New Kingdom. An imposing Ramesside temple and enclosure were built on the south-eastern part of the mound to protect against invasion. Settlement continued around the flanks of the site, which borehole surveys in the local fields show was surrounded by water for much of the year (Hughes 2007, Bunbury et al. 2014). Even though it was a defensive settlement, no moat was required since there was natural protection of the islands by water. Kom Firin continued to be inhabited for the next 1,500 years, during which there were periods of growth and revival.

After a period of political uncertainty, Psamtek I reunified Egypt under the nearby capital of Sais and Kom Firin experienced a renaissance. By this time, the northern branch of the waterway that had formerly enclosed the site seemed to have dwindled and the new enclosure was laid out on a much grander scale, expanding well beyond the earlier Ramesside enclosure that nestled in the south-east corner of the new enclosure. The evidence from a steep scarp to the south of the site and a relict lake along this front suggests that the settlement was still served by a waterway to the south for much of the year. Spencer (2014) concludes that at this time the community had grown from a frontier village to an established population of some tens of thousands who had limited connections to the nearby Greek trading emporion at Naukratis.

The town continued to thrive during Ptolemaic and Roman times and pottery has been reported from the site continuing until the Arab Conquest. During this period, the dwindling waterways of the delta (see Chapter 7) meant that the site became less attractive. Since the site was extensively mined for sebakh (organically rich silt), the paucity of later stonework and architecture can be attributed to the exposure of the latest periods of occupation to upcycling, particularly the production of lime and sebakh for fertiliser.

The management of the Nile's resources and effective irrigation of flood basins required co-ordination of groups of people up and down the Nile. Textual evidence suggests that the functions were co-ordinated by priests on behalf of the king, whose responsibility was to maintain 'maat' (the balance of things) and keep out the forces of chaos. The many texts of the walls of Edfu Temple were beautifully preserved by the occupation mound that grew over it and were later revealed by excavators in the early twentieth century (see Moeller 2010 for more detail). One religious journey to the Ptolemaic Temple of Edfu, described in the texts, is reminiscent of similar, independently conceived pilgrimages to manage water distribution like those of the Balinese water temples (Lansing 2007).

Horus of Edfu was host to an annual visit of the goddess Hathor, who travelled upstream from Dendara to Edfu in the south. The feast was placed in the middle of the agricultural season (Blackman and Fairman 1942) towards the end of the second month of Peret, after the planting and as the early growing season proceeded. As the goddess travelled upstream her retinue was augmented by representatives of towns along the Nile until the flotilla arrived at Edfu. By the time it arrived Edfu, the assembly would have included representatives from five successive nomes (ancient provinces).

At Edfu the goddess Hathor was closeted with the god Horus while the retinue feasted and participated in religious drama. The scenes enacted celebrated the triumph of Horus over his enemy Seth. First actors representing the demons and other enemies of Maat, the divine order of things, attempted to approach the temple by boat but were repelled by Horus and his supporters. The drama culminated with the dismemberment

FIGURE 9.8 Mud-brick fort at the Roman settlement of Umm el-Dabadib in the Kharga Basin. The fort is associated with a planned settlement of the same period as well as an earlier settlement of more informal layout

of Seth, apparently in the form of a hippopotamus modelled from bread (Blackman and Fairman 1942), to ensure that the next season of inundation was as successful as the current one had been. Blackman and Fairman also suggest that the extensive renditions of the dramatic texts, accompanied by lists of props and dialogue, were intended to continue the good work of maintaining order even if the physical ritual should cease.

Moderation of the climate meant additional activity in both the Western and Eastern deserts. Travelling and mining activity increased in both areas, while additional defence was required in the west to repel invaders entering Egypt through the oases. Dabadeb is a romantically ruined site deep in the desert of the Kharga Basin, part way between the springs of Ain Lebakh and Ain Amur on the route from Kharga to Dakhla (Figure 9.8). The site was active from prehistoric times as it was close to the ancient lake shore and, as the lake retreated, human activity followed the shoreline into a depression at the lowest point of the lake bed. There was a later renewal of activity during either the Second Intermediate Period or the New Kingdom, consisting of some dwellings and a temple (now demolished) associated with a sizeable

FIGURE 9.9 Recording a well in the Kharga Depression. Observations of sediment suggest that the well was a metre or so deep and surrounded by a low wall that protected it from sand incursion. Abundant pottery, broken at the site, testifies to its purpose

well (now dry). During Roman times a new settlement grew up, first informally and later a more formal square fort that, although not intended to be a defensive structure, being only one brick thick, was probably discouraging to would-be invaders. There were rich soils in the basin in which Dabadeb sat but water was sparse. Nonetheless, a large area of field systems is laid out in the muds of the ancient lake bed. To irrigate these, long lines of qanats were dug down through the lake mud as far as the local sandstone to collect groundwater percolating out of the rocks. Of the nine qanats at Dabadeb most are several kilometres long (Ikram and Rossi 2001), illustrating the effort that was required to glean water for these field systems. A brief effort was made to renew these qanats in the 1950s but the new settlement did not persist long.

More broadly, the landscape of the Kharga Basin was also dotted in Roman times with many houses, pigeon towers and wells. Major routes led through the desert via wells (Figure 9.9) and small areas of agriculture to mines (said by Beadnell 1909 to be for alum) and springs.

In the Eastern Desert, which is rich in metals and minerals, including carnelian, amethyst, gold and emeralds, activity also increased. An example of renewed interest in the Eastern Desert is the opening of the emerald mines of the Wadi Gimal, Wadi Nuqrus, Wadi Sikait and Gebel Zubara that all cluster around Gebel Zubara – the emerald mountain. These mines were used in Ptolemaic and Roman periods and then again in the Byzantine period (Shaw et al. 1999). A further brief period of exploitation during the Middle Ages was followed by some exploration under the auspices of Muhammad Ali but the quality of the emeralds could not rival those from Columbia discovered around 1500 AD.

The mine workings that remain from Ptolemaic times are focussed around productive lodes in the Wadi Gimal area, where they were probably worked by small expeditions. Ptolemaic rock-cut temples in the Wadi Sikait also suggest that this area was the target of early mining. At Wadi Gimal, minimal infrastructure was created, including some huts, sites for breaking the rock to extract minerals, a colonnaded building with a commanding view of the site and a small strongroom, probably for storing the products of the mine. As our understanding is that the desert was relatively wet at that period, the miners could supplement their stores with water and with game obtained locally. In Late Roman times, larger buildings were constructed and goods were imported to the mines in a very large number of amphorae whose refuse collected at the back of the mining settlement. The Wadi Sikait mine is dominated by generations of accumulated mineral tailings upon which later buildings rest only to be surrounded by subsequent deposits. A network of footpaths through the hills joined the active mines, which were supported by desert roads including way stations, watchtowers and hydreumata (fortified wells).

During the New Kingdom, the understanding and management of the Nile had developed but the sheer extent and complexity of tributary management during the Roman occupation enabled unprecedented growth and development of the empire. Roman technology maximised Egypt's capabilities commercially in the form of mineral trade and mining, and settlement expansion throughout previously uninhabitable lands. The milder climate allowed city dwellers to flourish because of previously unavailable produce and an abundance of grains, shipped up on barges, whilst farmers benefited from new markets. The eastern Mediterranean formed a marketplace of which Egypt was an important part. The development of new irrigation and water distribution strategies coupled with a beneficent climate brought the Nile to heel.

10

FROM COPTIC TO ISLAMIC TIMES:
A WELL-DOCUMENTED MOVEMENT
OF THE NILE FROM AL-FUSTAT
THROUGH BABYLON

ROMAN INNOVATIONS IN THE MANAGEMENT OF THE NILE established the patterns which persisted until the twentieth century. The ebb and flow of empires – Byzantine, Arab and Muslim – saw continued migration of the Nile accompanied by gentle rising of the floodplain.

Coptic Cairo is an excellent illustration of the interplay of floodplain rise and river migration. Early churches in the area, founded in the third to fourth century AD, are now far below the surrounding ground level. In another example, the 'Hanging Church' of St George was built over the bastions of an existing Roman watergate in the third to fourth century. Those original Roman bastions are now far below ground level and visitors must descend steps to go down from the modern floodplain level to the ancient one (Figure 10.1 and Sheehan 2015). The picture shows how St Barbara's Church in Cairo is now somewhat below ground level and must be reached by steps from a street level that is itself below the level of the surrounding landscape. The approximate rate of rise of around 1 m per millennium is clearly visible in the rising floor levels of successive foundations. Coptic Cairo and the adjacent Fustat, which formed the early part of the Islamic city, were originally on the Nile bank and incorporated quays; now, as a result of migration westwards, they have been left 500 m from the bank.

Nilometer records that had been kept so faithfully elsewhere began to be kept on the island of Roda in Cairo, where the nilometer (Figure 10.2) is famous for having records going back to the eighth century. Water entered from the river through the archway into the nilometer chamber. The chamber was furnished with steps for access and a central calibrated pillar from which the flood-level rise could be monitored. Although it has suffered damage during this period and been renovated many times, the original nilometer is thought to have been built around 715 AD (www.waterhistory .org/histories/cairo/). Cairo itself has had many centres and Mark Lehner

FIGURE 10.1 Entrance to St Barbara's Church in Coptic Cairo

proposes that we should rather think of the Cairo area as a 'capital zone', with migrating centres that were, in part, dependent upon the location of the Nile within the valley. Early construction seems to be mainly in the Saqqara and Giza areas in the Old Kingdom, when we infer that the Nile or at least a western branch of it was towards that side of the valley. The easterly site of Heliopolis was also at that time on a branch of the Nile, and from this Pryer (2011) has proposed that the delta head, where the branching of the Nile began, was further to the south than it is now.

FIGURE 10.2 Roda Nilometer, Cairo, from the Nile

From the 13th Dynasty (c. 1800–1650 BC) the delta came under new management, that of the Hyksos (rulers of foreign lands), who by the 15th Dynasty had largely taken control of the area. The emergence of the southern capital, Thebes, during the Middle and New Kingdom resulted in a power struggle for the delta, which was finally 're-Egyptianised' during the early 18th Dynasty. This conquest was accompanied by the construction of fortifications such as those at Kom Firin (Spencer 2014) on one of the geziereh (turtle-backs). Although the channels and the areas between the turtle-backs continued to dry out, the locations of former channels were still visible in maps from the chains of swampy land and minor lakes that marked their former progress until the late nineteenth century. During the period of Mohammad Ali, canals were cut to drain the swamps and regulate the flow of water for irrigation and the earlier pattern of channels was overwritten. A second period of water management began in more contemporary times, such as during the leadership of Nasser.

Burgeoning trade with the eastern Mediterranean during the New Kingdom had led to the development of ports along the delta fringes and these links continued into the Coptic and Islamic periods. Suitable port locations relied upon a supply of fresh water, some of which may have been delivered from a source further upstream, and good access to sea-ward routes and inland connections through the waterways of the delta. John Cooper's (2014) study presents a fascinating insight into the Nile as a working, dynamic river, charting its importance during the Islamic period for cultural, navigational and trade purposes. Tinnis, an important textile production and trading port, was said to have become an island during the earthquake of 365 AD (Gascoigne 2007) and continued to be used until the thirteenth century. Exploratory borehole work by Ben Pennington suggests that Tinnis was founded on a number of shelly ridges, produced by long-shore drift eastwards along the coast of Egypt. When Attia (1954) bored in this area he reported muds containing cockle shells supporting this hypoth-esis. Longshore drift distributed sediment from the Damietta branch of the Nile across the mouth of the lagoon enclosing the marine cockle spits and the city of Tinnis sprang from the archipelago. The principal sailing season was during the summer when the weather was stable (Tammuz 2005) and the floodwaters were higher, filling the lagoon.

Trade goods were produced during the Mamluk period across Egypt and, at times, made use of extensive irrigation works to produce the crops desired. Agricultural basins of this type occur at Shutb, just south of Asyut, and at Akhmin, both well known for their textiles. At Asyut, a system of dykes was created to form the Zinnar Basin, to control irrigation of an area around 150 km². The crops grown in this area are unrecorded but the investment in cre-ating the dykes included up to two hundred oxen and many men labouring to create a lightly baked brick double wall with an earth filling. The import-ance of the indigo trade (Balfour-Paul 2016) as well as the export of blue-dyed cloth from Asuyt to central Africa at that time suggest that a species of tropical indigo was part of the purpose of the irrigation. Augering in the area of Shutb (ancient Shas-Hotep) within the basin revealed that around 3.5 m of sediment had accumulated during the period of intense agricul-ture, a rate that exceeds the normal rates of accumulation. The provisions for maintaining the Mamluk wall included its maintenance and defence, a further indication of the value of the crop.

Further to the north, the changing geometry of the river meant that what is now southern Cairo became more suitable for the pre-eminent settle-ment in the area than the earlier sites of the capital further to the south-west, including Memphis. The earliest part of this new capital is in Old Cairo (ancient Babylon), which still has the remains of a Roman watergate upon which the Greek Orthodox Church has built the 'Hanging Church' of St George. The ground level of the Roman gate towers is now around 6 m below the ground level of modern Cairo, illustrating the effect of both floodplain rise and the accretion of occupied sites. Other religious buildings grew up around this area, including St Barbara's, founded in the fifth or sixth century AD, and the Ben Ezra Synagogue, home of the Cairo Genizah, where century-old manuscripts accumulated between around 870 AD and the nineteenth century. Some 200,000 documents preserved in the Genizah shed light on the development of the area. Shortly after the Muslim conquest of Egypt in 641 AD, Al-Fustat was founded a little further north on a sandstone shelf towards the eastern side of the Nile canyon (Levanoni 2008).

By the medieval period the city centre had again moved further north. The walled city was centred on the Al-Azhar Mosque, still close to the Nile bank, and received water through a system of channels and reservoirs that protected the city from devastation during the flood. Unfortunately, the presence of Al-Fustat, a little further upstream, was deleterious to the water quality and required water to be brought from further away and for purification of various kinds. Between the tenth and the fourteenth centuries the Nile migrated further westwards, making the provision of water more difficult, although the city became safer from flooding. In the late fourteenth century, the earlier port was replaced by a new port at Bulaq to the northwest of the old city. The modern centre of Cairo is still further downstream again and the point at which the delta begins to branch is now another 20 km further downstream.

Islamic influence also stretched further north into the delta, with a network of waterways, described in detail by John Cooper (2014), being extended and maintained. This included straightening and deepening existing channels of the distributary to make them suitable for navigation, albeit by shallow draft boats, as well as the creation of cross-branch links to connect the lagoons and branches (Figure 10.3). Continuous sedimentation meant that the work required continuous attention if the waterway was to remain in use and, in some cases, resulted in such high embankments of dredged silt that sailing became impossible since they had taken the wind. Among these projects was a renewal of the connection to the Red Sea, a 170 km connection starting at Babylon and joining the Bitter Lakes to the north-western inlet of the Red Sea.

Barrages or embankments constructed from sunken boats and stone were also used to revet channel banks and possibly to provide weirs that could conserve navigation upstream of the weir. Throughout the whole of the time since the unification of Egypt, strategies to protect the capital from inundation and to ensure a supply of fresh water and sufficient irrigation for crops were essential to the survival of the country. The focus of the leaders' efforts, while not defending the territory from external threats, was to retain

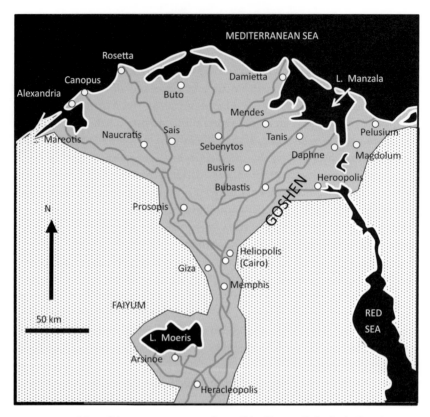

FIGURE 10.3 Map of the transport connections of the Eastern Delta including the Bitter Lakes canal taken from a historical map of the Nile Delta (Shepherd 1911)

and restore order. The disastrous consequence of failing to retain a balance is illustrated by Bedouin raids into the Nile Valley during the Ottoman period. The raids were intended to disrupt irrigation schemes and thus extend the grazing lands upon which their stock depended. However, the effect on the seat of power in the Cairo area was disastrous since too much sediment and water came down during the flood, motivating punitive expeditions to the south to restore control of irrigation. This illustrates the way in which habitation of the Nile Valley required co-operation along its length and much of this organisation was conducted by the king or his representatives.

Although we have relatively little detail of who attended and how the ancient works for the preservation of Maat were conducted, there is plenty of information to construct an outline of the process and there may be strong continuity between these ancient rites and modern festivals. For example, the Early Dynastic Scorpion Mace Head from Hierakonpolis shows the King Scorpion by a canal brandishing a hoe and ready to break the banks to release the irrigation water, while the later Ptolemaic temple at Edfu contains a large number of detailed texts that deal with the duties and religious dramas associated with the work of the king (see Chapter 9). Recently curated film by the Bibliotheca Alexandrina of the Moulid Abu al-Haggag has captured a religious procession from the old mosques of Luxor to the Abu al-Haggag Mosque at Luxor. The procession includes boats in full sail (mounted on wheels) as well as lorries with improvised sails, suggesting continuity from the deep past of the New Kingdom festivals held in Luxor, particularly the Festival of Opet where the barque shrines of Amun and his retinue made their way to Luxor Temple and back.

In the annual cycle as well as longer cycles there emerge a number of phases: flooding, greening, harvesting and desiccation. From the earliest unification of Egypt, the annual cycle was well understood. This knowledge formed the basis for the Coptic calendar and was closely monitored by the Egyptian state using nilometers. The calendar was divided into three seasons: Akhet (June to September), Peret (October to February) and Shemu (March to May). In the first phase, Akhet, the river started to rise in the south, and the flood travelled north over the following weeks. As the river rose, levees were strategically breached to irrigate flood basins and the inhabitants were forced to retreat to high ground, including the flanking terraces of the Nile Valley, river levees and, in the delta, ancient sandbanks known as gezireh (islands). A flood too low was disastrous and resulted in famine, while one too high caused widespread disruption of irrigation networks and dwellings. Prayers were directed towards a rise of 16 cubits (Figure 10.4), neither too little nor too much, and taxes were set accordingly. Ancient accounts tell of the flooding of Karnak Temple and Roman papyri from Oxyrhynchus (Parsons 2007) describe the emergency measures used when an embankment was accidentally breached, including men and furniture pressing into the gap while earth could be recruited to stem the flow.

Having welcomed the flood, there was a wait of a month or more until it began to recede and the land could be prepared for agriculture, the season of Peret. The Ottoman traveller Evliyya Çelebi, during his visit to Egypt in 1672–80, described the festivities when the flood began to recede as well as the frenzied activity that ensued as fresh mud emerged from the water. So busy were people brick-making and preparing for agriculture that he described there being 'no place to drop a needle' (Çelebi 1938).

As kemet, the Black Land as the ancient Egyptians knew it, emerged once again from the floodwaters, the agricultural season, Shemu, began.

FIGURE 10.4 A Graeco-Roman sculpture (with replacement head) of the Nile god surrounded by putti representing the 16 cubits of flood raise required for the ideal harvest

Although in the oases a local supply of artesian water meant that there could be year-round agriculture, in general in the Nile Valley there was a relatively short growing and harvesting season; as the land dried out, the season of preparation began. Again, we know from Roman accounts (Parsons 2007) of duties shirked, that a labour tax was exacted from each able-bodied member of the community so that the cleaning, digging of ditches and repair of embankments could be effected before the floodwaters rose and the cycle began again. Indeed, to garner sufficient food, in anticipation of the inactivity of the flood season, it was crucial to improve irrigation and productivity as far as possible. Since grain was the main currency, bread and beer being the standard payment from the Old Kingdom (2686–2160 BC), and was taxed, the state invested a good deal in the expansion of irrigation. Juan Carlos Garcea Moreno (personal communication) suggests from the records that marginal marshes and swamps were an important source of fish, fowl and game – an alternative larder upon which the population drew more heavily when state intervention was weaker (see also Chapter 4).

The involvement of a network of priests and scholars to monitor and measure the Nile and its behaviour reached a new zenith in the time of Mohammad Ali, who imported engineers, doctors and other experts from all over Egypt and the Near East to produce a regional Nile management scheme.

MODERN CHANGES TO EGYPT: DAMS
AND IRRIGATION: CAN WE EVER
CONTROL THE NILE?

A MAJOR CHANGE TO WATER MANAGEMENT CAME WITH THE LEAD-
ership of Muhammad Ali in the early nineteenth century. A subject
of the Ottoman Empire and raised in what is now Greece from Albanian
descent, Muhammad Ali aspired to create a modern European-style state in
Egypt and imported European ideas of science and medicine. The particular
effect on the hydrology of the Nile was the imposition of a country-wide
strategy for agriculture and the attendant construction of barrages and canals
to enable this to happen.

Mohammad Ali's reforms in irrigation and medicine produced a rapid
expansion in population, and new villages founded along the Nile banks
at that time are still visible today on GoogleEarth images (Figure 11.1).
Although Mohammad Ali had planned to start a programme of railway
building, it was his successor, Abbas I, who ultimately commissioned Robert
Louis Stephenson to build the first railway. Railways required embankments,
particularly in the marshy lands of the delta, and paired projects of canal excavation and embankment building brought water to new parts of the delta
and straightened existing waterways. A late nineteenth-century barrage at
Aswan started to reduce the extremes of the Nile flood and in the 1960s this
was extended to form the Aswan High Dam, which still maintains the Nile
around a median level year round. A study by Katy Lutley of Nile migration, which is controlled by the amount of water passing through the river
system, suggests that net migration rates since the construction of the dam
are similar to those before. However, the migration is now spread through
the year, where much of it was previously focussed into the flood season.

The raising of the High Dam meant that settlements were no longer
restricted to patches of high ground. Villages expanded across the floodplain
and Cairo, freed from constraint, is now a megacity that straddles the entire
Nile Valley and is developing satellite cities in the desert beyond. The end of
the flood has increased the capacity of agricultural land to grow year-round

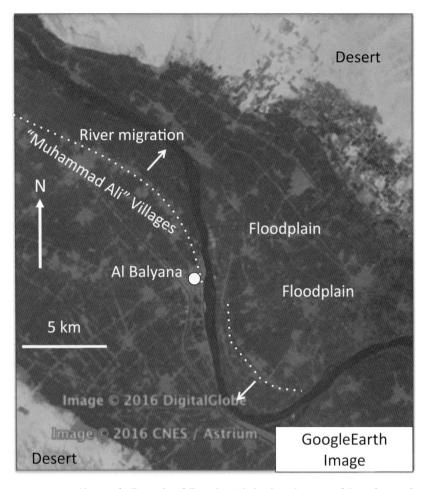

FIGURE 11.1 Chains of villages that follow the Nile bank at the time of the reforms of Mohammad Ali

crops but has placed constraints on irrigation and fertility. In the late nineteenth century, farmers were given permission to use accumulations of nutrient-rich mud brick and organic debris from old sites to fertilise their fields, which no longer received so much nourishing silt. This organic-rich material is known locally as sebakh and forms the koms or tells of the settlement mounds. Given that there are so many ancient sites in Egypt it is readily available and, in places such as Edfu and El-Kab in southern Egypt among others, a huge volume of material was quarried to spread onto the neighbouring fields. In the process many artefacts and, in the case of

Edfu, an entire temple was revealed for the edification of Egyptologists and archaeologists and to the delight of the many travellers who were starting to come to Egypt with Cook's Tours. Stones revealed were recycled in new buildings often with no reference to their original design or distributed through the antiquities market. Marble and limestone blocks could be burnt for lime, resulting in the denudation of Roman remains from sites such as Kom Firin (see Chapter 9).

Some farmers, recognising that the koms were fertile, planted crops on them, although this was not possible where the land was formally recognised as an antiquities site. Hence, sweet potatoes are often found growing today on the mounds of old unrecognised sites in the delta since the potatoes like the high phosphorus content of the ancient refuse. In some cases, large quantities of sebakh were extracted and distributed across the land. In borehole cores around Kom Firin and the small site of Kom el-Farahy near Edfu, sediment and pottery from the excavated mound were found to have spread several hundred metres from the site and to have been ploughed over time into the top 1.5 m of the sediment. Stan Hendrickx and his colleagues (2010) studied the quarrying of El-Kab, documenting extensive removal of mud from the large excavation mound there as sebakh. Indeed, finding that the mud was exceedingly rich in pottery, the farmers wished to remove the sherds from the sebakh. Eventually such a large accumulation of sherds remained that it was used as ballast on the railway.

Among Mohammad Ali's reforms the combination of improved medical care, particularly for women, and management of agriculture meant that from a low of only three million people around 1800 (Cohen 1995) Egypt's population has grown to its current ninety million (2016). Pressure on current settlements means that agricultural land continues to be developed for housing and the adjacent deserts to be regreened (Figure 11.2). Once again humans in Egypt are changing the landscape to support themselves.

Another way of expanding the irrigable area of Egypt is the development of the New Valley Project. Where the ancient Khargan Lake overflowed, excavation has reactivated the ancient natural Toshka spillway to provide additional agricultural land. Boreholes supplying large rotor arms (Figure 11.3) are springing up across the desert as the raised water level in Lake Nasser refreshes the fossil waters in the Nubian aquifer, raising the groundwater level across the Saharan region.

The downside of all this irrigation can be a loss of water from areas further down the irrigation system and the salination of soils as salt accumulates from evaporating water. For example, around 2004 Lake Qarun in the

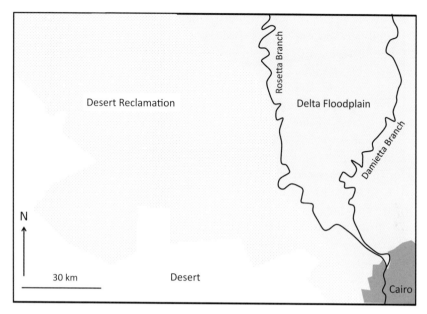

FIGURE 11.2 Diagram drawn from historic GoogleEarth imagery showing how the expansion of the delta fringes proceeded during the twentieth century

Faiyum turned red from the accumulation of salts and fertiliser. The water supply to the lake has now been increased to raise the shoreline and reduce the salinity by dilution. The remediation of agricultural plots that are saline includes using desert sand laid over the soil to wick up the salt so that it can be physically removed with the sand. Ancient low-salinity and high-fertility soils, for example those around Luxor that are overlain by wadi-wash gravels, are being excavated to provide new field plots.

In the north, the delta is also threatened by climate change and the attendant sea-level rise in the Mediterranean (Figure 11.4); since most sediment is currently retained in Lake Nasser, the delta is unable to rebuild itself. As it sinks under the weight of its own sediment no fresh sediment is brought by the river. Towards the coast, the delta lagoons continue gradually to fill, assisted by fish farmers who enclose and manage the shallow parts of the lake. Longshore drift in the Mediterranean continues to shape the coastal ridge of the delta, eroding old mouths of the Nile and shifting sand anti-clockwise around the eastern Mediterranean. Meanwhile a new delta is forming in the south of Lake Nasser that itself can be an agricultural area. Whether the growth of this delta can continue now that new dams on the Nile in Sudan are being commissioned remains to be seen.

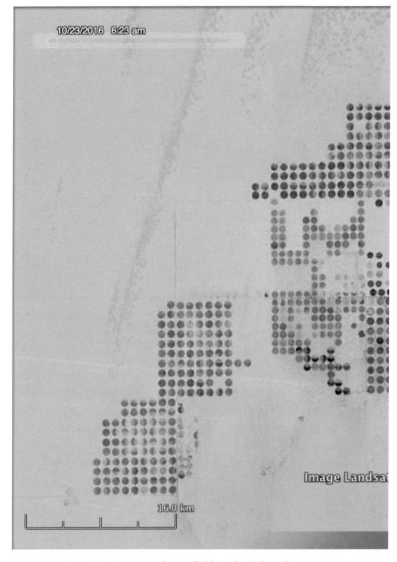

10/23/2016 6:23 am

Image Landsat

16.0 km

FIGURE 11.3 GoogleEarth image of rotor fields in the Sahara Desert

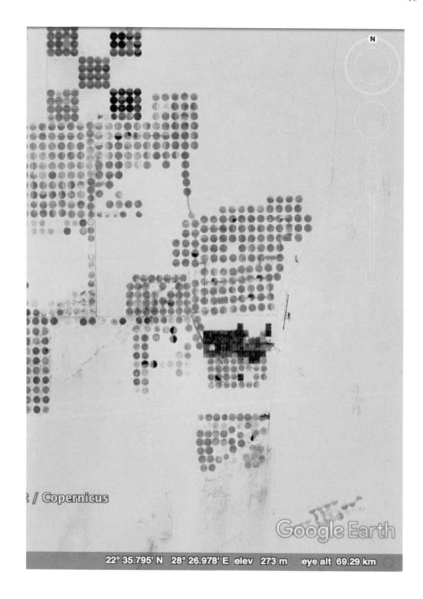

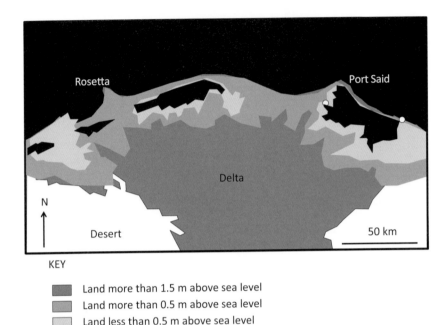

KEY

Land more than 1.5 m above sea level
Land more than 0.5 m above sea level
Land less than 0.5 m above sea level
Sea

FIGURE 11.4 Diagram from United Nations Environmental Programme (UNEP) estimates of the extent to which the delta will be flooded with 0.5 m and 1.5 m of sea-level rise

Many of these changes are boons to the archaeologist, revealing unsuspected remains of the past, but they are also changing and concealing forever the legacy of millennia of ancient dialogue between the Nile and its inhabitants. Mercifully, modern geophysical techniques supported by recent and historical satellite and air photography imagery when allied with ground-truthing mean that there is still a wealth of information that can be extracted from any football field or garden. The Nile continues to respond to the changes imposed upon it. Climate oscillations, as they have so many times before, will regreen the desert or enhance its aridity, leading to new human responses. What we do know is that in Egypt the past will be a blueprint for the landscape changes of the future.

APPENDIX

Landscape Interpretation Tips

Reading the Nile's Progress from Satellite Images and Sediments

Given that all sites in the Nile Valley may have been affected by Nile migration, there are a number of methods for assessing the likely movements of the Nile in the area. After the initial assessment, strategic augering (boreholes) can be used to test the sediments, determining the time frame of the movements. A number of techniques have been developed since the availability of good satellite imagery from GoogleEarth; other techniques add data available from digital elevation models (DEMs) and historic declassified Corona Satellite images that recorded landscapes before large-scale construction and irrigation projects of the late twentieth century. Recent release of Landsat8 data can also reveal useful information, such as the presence of gypsum crusts in the desert that are indicative of playa lakes.

There are a number of stages of assessment and investigation of sites, starting with identification of koms and hod (field-group) boundaries on GoogleEarth, moving through processing of DEMs and multi-spectral imagery (Parcak 2009) to field-walking, geophysical investigation and ultimately an augering campaign to understand the development of the sites with respect to the Nile or other channels in space and time. At each stage, the investigation requires a greater investment and greater focus.

GoogleEarth Assessment

Most sites in Egypt are visible in GoogleEarth. The hod or field-group boundaries around them have remained relatively conservative for a number of reasons. The first is that, before the construction of the High Dam at Aswan, the Nile Valley was flooded by the monsoon rains from Ethiopia and only high points in the floodplain (turtle-backs of Pleistocene sand, river levees and terraces that flanked the Nile Valley) remained inhabitable by the population. Thus higher, occupied areas tended to remain high due to anthropogenic aggradation and hence could continue to be occupied. The second is that the inundated farmland was redivided after the flood by the village dalal (a local surveyor) who used former levees and other features to divide up field groups that could subsequently be divided into strips. Finally, the road network and irrigation channels worked in symbiosis with the river levees to retain their height above the flood as the floodplain rose. Sediment that collected in the canals was regularly dredged and helped to keep the adjacent roadways and canal levees above the general level of the flood.

Augering

While many different methods of augering exist, in practice one of the most suitable for conditions in Egypt is often the Eijkelkamp hand auger (or Dutch auger). Its main advantages are that it is light and easily transported, can be operated in restricted spaces including in archaeological excavations and is minimally invasive. The limitations of this kind of auger are that it does not retrieve a continuous core and cannot penetrate consolidated sediments. Hence many archaeologists have added augering to the battery of tools that they can use to explore the subsurface around sites.

A typical set of augering equipment includes a range of augering heads adapted to the retrieval of different sediments (Figure A.1). The photograph shows how a handle and a sampling barrel are joined by 1-m rods. Insertion of additional rods means that the auger can bore up to around 8 m in Nile silt although longer cores of up to 16 m have been recorded. With a general raise of floodplain of 1 m per millennium, these 8 to 10 metres may represent as much as ten thousand years of history. Alternative barrels, suitable for different types of sediment, are in the storage tube in the middle ground of the photo and attached via a system of raised buttons and sleeves to a handle used to turn the head. Coarser sediments can be recovered with larger, more open heads, while muds and clays require a smaller more closed head. These heads can generally retrieve sediments from 20 cm of coring coarse materials to 5 cm of fine materials. Other accessories include a screw head for passing stones, a corkscrew-like 'stone catcher' and a baler to remove excess water from the borehole. To case the hole and prevent down-hole contamination, plastic tube lengths joined by screw-threads are used to line the borehole. Casing can also be used to pass through coarse sand bodies that are prone to collapse into the borehole, particularly below the water table. Alternatively, these may be passed by shaking the auger to make the sand/water mix liquefy and then jabbing down to a mud layer below it.

FIGURE A.1 Eijkelkamp hand auger

Concerns raised with the interpretation of material retrieved by augering include observations that the artefacts are 'out of context'. While it is true that they are not in the context of a room or floor deposit, they may equally be regarded as being in the context of the swamp, river or other waterbody revealed by the sedimentary evidence. Whilst bioturbation of the sediments is common, as is evidence of plant growth in the form of rhizocretions, these intrusions are generally on the millimetre to centimetre scale and do not disturb the overall stratigraphy. Typical sedimentary layers in Egypt are river sediments, which form beds on a decimetre to metre scale, and flood and over-bank deposits, which are on a centimetre to decimetre scale. Exceptions to this are fine flood laminae, which are often preserved but which may be blurred by bioturbation, and the plough layer which, given long-term agriculture in the Nile Valley, can affect the upper metre or two of the sediments, destroying sedimentary structure. A final confounding factor is down-hole contamination, which can be eliminated by continuous casing of the borehole. Where casing is not practicable, contamination can be minimised by monitoring the progress of the head downwards during augering, since large amounts of fallen material arrest the progress of drilling.

FIGURE A.2 Tray of clasts sieved out of an auger core

From the sediments retrieved from augering, attributes such as colour, grain size and sorting reveal the watery environment of the deposition, be it a fast-flowing river that produces sandy sediments or, at the other end of the scale, the anoxic (dark and smelly) mud that accumulates in stagnant water. In addition to the geological information, archaeological information is also found within the cores, which may include fragments of pottery, chippings of building stone, residues of bone and many more items often thrown into the water, particularly around harbours, settlements and canal banks (Figure A.2). In the photograph, the majority of the items are pottery fragments but there are also two angular white limestone chips and a rounded pale sandstone fragment, typical of material from the Gebel Silsila sandstone quarries. While care must be taken in interpreting these deposits, archaeological items are often so numerous (up to five hundred per core) as to provide a sequence of dates by which the sediment had formed, as new 'species' of inclusion join the assemblage through time, a process described by geologists as 'sequence stratigraphy'. When added to information from the archaeological sites around the former waterbody, such as the footprints of buildings with time, it is possible to construct a sequence of successive landscapes as the sedimentary processes develop.

As augering is a relatively intensive method of obtaining data it is most effective when used in conjunction with other methods of exploration. As a guideline, a team of six can auger and analyse around 10 m of core in a working day. The sites of auger cores can be strategically located if a preliminary examination of maps, historical maps, air photographs and satellite images is used to evaluate how the landscape has changed with time. The results of a cartographic survey can be extrapolated to provide a geometry but often no precise timescale for past landscape change. The surface survey can be further extended by incorporation of archaeological data from monuments in the region, which can normally be assumed to have remained on mostly dry land since the time of their construction. Geophysical methods can also be used to add a component of subsurface stratigraphy, in particular electric resistance tomography, which can be used to extend surface observations into three dimensions.

To add a further dimension to this three-dimensional model, strategic augering (particularly where the auger site is less than 50 m from a settlement) can add time constraints to the 3D dataset.

Sediments associated with deposition in the Nile are often modified by human activity around archaeological sites, but the archaeological materials that are incorporated in the cores reveal chronological information about the changing environment. Bunbury and Jeffreys (2005) in the Survey of Memphis and Bunbury et al. (2008) found that anthropogenic material (mainly pottery) is often abundant in cores close to sites (up to 30 per cent of the sediment) but there is little evidence that it travels more than 50 m from the site due to the hydrodynamics of broken pottery, which means that sherds tend to become quickly incorporated into the sediment.

Types of Sediment Found in Egypt

The grain size of the sediment sampled is indicative of the speed of the water flowing when it was deposited. As the water accelerates, successively larger grain sizes are incorporated into the waterbody, leaving a lag of larger items at the base of the channel. As the water decelerates the grains are deposited again, such that the larger-grained sands are deposited before finer-grained silt and finally clay. In this way, the main channel of the Nile is dominated by beds that have coarse, yellow sand towards the bottom of the unit and brown silts towards the top, while minor channels contain silts and clay. A typical thickness of one of these units in the main channel is 1–2 m but other deposits are thinner. Since the whole unit can be considered as a single event that has occurred in a matter of a few days (or less) the lag (gravel) can be used to determine the date of the whole unit. The beds are thinnest

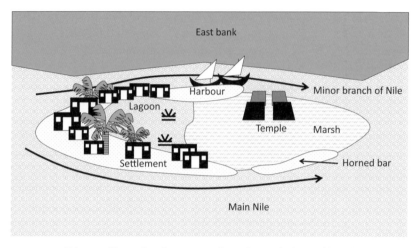

FIGURE A.3 Diagram illustrating the topography and use of a horned bar developing in the Nile Valley

in stagnant backwaters where the sediment is deposited very slowly and are composed of fine clay. Since oxygen cannot easily permeate such fine-grained deposits, these units are often anoxic, making them dark grey with a distinctive, unpleasantly sulphurous smell.

Taryn Duckworth (2009) studied a number of islands in the Karnak area and discerned that there is a typical sequence of island formation and development in the Nile. Initially a sandbar or a sequence of bars forms. As water divides to go around the bar, sandy flanks form on either side of the core to form a horned bar (Figure A.3). Within the core of the horned bar, shallow, still water means that fish favour the centres while vegetation tends to colonise the upper surface. This vegetation stabilises the bar and baffles further sediment, meaning that the bar grows. It was at this point during island formation that villagers in the Karnak area started to colonise the island, placing any residences and crops on the upstream part of the bar that rises furthest above the water and driving stock through the shallows to graze, churn and fertilise the vegetation on the rest of the island. As the island is increasingly consolidated, further colonisation can occur with larger plants taking hold on the island. With time, the minor channel fills with sediment and one end of the bar joins to the mainland. Gradually the minor channel fills until the old island is bonded to the mainland. By this time, new islands and horned bars have usually already spawned and the process can begin again.

The other method of deposition on the floodplain occurs when the river floods and causes the formerly fast-flowing sediments to be released suddenly. They then become static; sand drops from the water almost immediately, while silt and clay will only settle slowly to fertilise the land. These deposits are usually only a few centimetres thick but may reach a maximum of 10–15 cm. Normal agricultural activity generally mixes these deposits together soon after they are formed.

Many different types of items have been observed in sediments from Egypt, including beads, teeth, bones, plant materials, chips of precious and building stones and many pot sherds. Closer examination of these items, which are particularly abundant in the basal lag, reveals much about the adjacent settlement, including the type of activity at the site and an indication of the time period within which it occurred. The abrasion of the objects also gives an indication of how long they have spent in transport before becoming part of the sediment. In addition, we find that some types of pottery are prone to rotting when they rest near the sediment/water interface and this is a useful indicator of the speed of burial and hence the environment.

Al-Zaniyah, a former island 2 km north of Karnak, was investigated in detail to give a background description of sediments typical of islands in the Nile. Evidence for Al-Zaniyah having been an island is provided by the local toponym for the hod (land parcel), Hod el-Gezireh ('island parcel'), and from eyewitness accounts of the area having been separated from the east bank by a wadeable channel in the 1950s before the construction of the Aswan High Dam. A section through the sediments of the channel that is around 50 m wide and a maximum of 5 m deep is given in Figure A.4. The cores AS18-21 were taken along a track crossing agricultural land. AS18 shows the intercalated sands and silts typical of the river levee and is situated at the outside of the bend. The sandy deposits of AS23, AS22 and AS19 indicate the main flow of the channel, which was deepest at AS22 where the sand bodies are both coarser-grained and thicker. Coarsening-upward deposits at the base of AS20 indicated the progradation (expansion) of the original island flanks, while AS21, currently close to the farm, shows how the interior of the island gradually infilled with muds deposited during times of quiet water and sands deposited during times of higher river flow.

The sediments are characteristic of a Nile environment with fining-upwards packages of Nile silt that coarsen towards the outside of the channel bend where the waterflow was fastest. At the very edge of the channel, levees are formed as water slowed by contact with the banks drops its coarsest fraction of sediment. In the lowest part of the channel, coarse sand is found in the bed load of the river, while there is a complex sequence of silts, sands and clays towards the inside of the bend that form broadly coarsening-upwards packages. These sequences are indicative of a set of accreting sandbars that

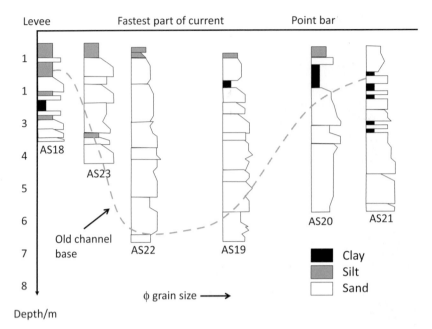

FIGURE A.4 Cross-section through the sediments of the historic channel at al-Zaniyah Island (now joined to the mainland)

typically form on the inside of the bend. The farmhouse is situated on the minor branch of the Nile towards the upstream end of the island, a site favoured also for habitation in antiquity. Since its time as an island, the minor channel has waned and gradually filled with sediment, and the island has become bonded to the Nile bank. Meanwhile, continued island formation has created a more recent island, now also bonded to the east bank, and yet another new island has formed in the channel. By this mechanism of sequential island formation and capture, the main Nile channel has moved a considerable distance over the past century, around 300 m in this case. A similar example occurs further south at Banana Island, now also no longer an island (Figure A.5). Katy Lutley's fastest migration rates (see Chapter 8) were for just such a setting – island capture close to a bend in the river.

Windblown Sand

In addition to the waterlain silts of the Nile Valley, windblown sand is also common in Egypt, forming large dune fields that move across the desert at 10 m per year or more (Figure A.6). Reconstructions of the past climate in Egypt and North Africa (Kuper and Kröpelin 2006, Kröpelin et al. 2008)

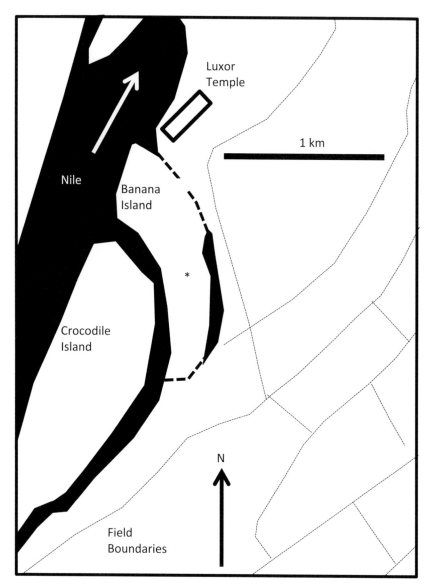

FIGURE A.5 Crocodile Island and the former Banana Island in the Luxor area, with the Nile to the west and the fields of the Nile floodplain to the east

FIGURE A.6 Contemporary active dune in the Sahara Desert showing a characteristic crescent shape and many small ripples on the surface

show that over the past ten thousand years the climate has changed from relatively wet to very arid. As rains continued to fail, desert vegetation that had flourished during warmer climes died, destabilising and releasing fossil sand dunes. Some of this sand has inevitably collected along the west scarp of the Nile Valley at sites such as Abusir (Chapter 4) and Dashur (Alexanian et al. 2012 and Chapter 5).

Sebakh

The completion of the first Aswan Dam in the late nineteenth century had an unwelcome side effect on local agriculture: it diminished the annual flood deposits, essential for keeping the soil fertile. Ancient sites, however, contain silt, and due to the debris incorporated into them are often rich in organic materials, which would have been invaluable to farmers as a fertiliser. So, from the construction of the dam until the end of the Second World War, permission was given for the extraction of silty material from ancient sites in Egypt (sebakh) and its subsequent use as a fertiliser (Bailey 1999). The practice was eventually stopped since large parts of settlement mounds were being destroyed in the process, for example at Edfu (see also

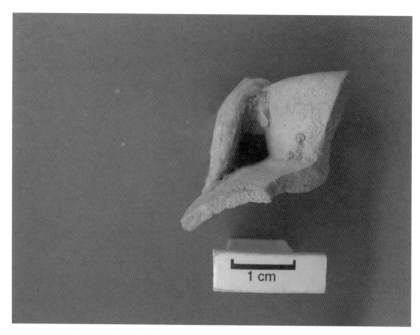

FIGURE A.7 Rim and handle of a Roman juglet (Sally-Ann Ashton personal communication) from a borehole core at Karnak (photo Angus Graham)

Chapter 11), where large quarries embayed the north and south of the town mound (Hendrickx 2010). The application of sebakh or silt-quarrying leaves a characteristic trace in borehole cores, with the addition of material rich in pottery and other materials being added to the fields and mixed by ploughing into the upper metre of the sediment column.

Pottery Series Dating

There is abundant pottery excavated at sites, in grave fields and in the sediments of the Nile Valley (Figure A.7). Petrie's early descriptions of Pre-Dynastic tombs allowed him to construct a series of types of pottery vessel (forms) that could be used to date assemblages that had no other evidence of period. Novelty in some types of ceramics seems to have been prized throughout Egyptian history and many types of pottery can be localised to a period, for example the Meidum bowls that are typical of the Old Kingdom and whose form in terms of diameter and rim shape is the frequent subject of ancient innovation. We might make a similar comparison for the twentieth century, when specific ceramics are readily recognised as originating in the 1950s or 1970s, for example. These ancient innovations in pottery form, coupled with their abundance in excavations and the exceptional expertise of the ceramicists working in Egypt, mean that greater precision is generally possible from ceramic indicators than from, for example, carbon dating. When studies of the fabric (internal structure) of the pottery are included, pottery analysis is a precise means of dating and correlating sediments and sites as well as identifying the types of activity that were conducted at them. For example, domestic wares indicate habitation while pottery kiln slag may indicate industrial activity.

GLOSSARY

Acheulean   An early archaeological industry and the first standardised tradition of tool-making amongst early humans, dating from between 1.5 million and 200,000 years ago. The tools are made of stone and characterised by pear- and oval-shaped hand axes.

Aeolian   Any process by which wind shapes the surface of the earth and changes a landscape. Such processes could be by erosion, transportation and deposition of sediment.

Aestivation   A state of animal dormancy (similar in nature to hibernation) during arid, hot periods to avoid damage, injury and desiccation from high temperatures.

Barque   A type of boat with significant religious meaning in ancient Egypt. A sailing vessel depicted with three or more masts and the fore- and mainmasts rigged square, it was the method of transportation of the deceased to the afterworld and carried the dead pharaoh to become a deity.

Birket   A natural or artificial place where water is collected and stored.

Corona images   A series of air photographs taken in the mid-twentieth century. Many are now available through historic imagery on GoogleEarth.

Debitage   The waste material produced in the manufacture of stone tools and implements, including different kinds of lithic flakes and blades, shatter and production debris and production rejects.

Deflation
The erosive process by which wind carries loose material from dry, flat areas and deposits them elsewhere, often hundreds of kilometres away, leading to deflation hollows or blowouts and the reduction of the level of desert surfaces.

Diorite
A relatively rare, dark white peppered, igneous rock formed through the crystallisation of magma beneath the Earth's crust.

Doline
A hollow or hole in the ground, frequently funnel-shaped, formed by the collapse of the surface layer, usually due to chemical dissolution. Also known as a sinkhole.

Epi-Palaeolithic
A term relating to the Stone Age hunter-gatherers who lived at the end of the Upper Palaeolithic but were distinct from the Mesolithic. The period is generally dated from 20,000 to 10,500 BP.

Genizah
A repository (often attached to a synagogue) for storing Jewish books and writings prior to their proper burial, following the law that forbids the throwing away of writings that contain the name of God.

Gezireh
Sand hill, formerly surrounded by the sea, which was naturally inhabited by the ancient Egyptians as a place of refuge during periods of flooding and deluge. Gezireh means 'island' in Arabic.

Ground-truthing
The process of validation of data, theories and ideas through direct observation by checking 'on the ground' or 'in the field'.

Hamsin
Dry, hot, sandy local wind, blowing from the south.

Hod
A land parcel defined by local landmarks. Individual fields for farming were laid out within the hod boundaries by a village surveyor after the recession of the annual flood.

Holocene	The geological epoch that began after the Pleistocene at around 11,700 BP when the last ice age ended and the glaciers retreated. It is a period characterised by warmer climate and vast developments in human knowledge and technology.
Induration	The hardening of rocks by heat or baking but may also include other hardening processes without the introduction of heat.
Kom	A word interchangeable with the Arabic word 'tell', meaning a mound or raised up area made up from the ruins of ancient settlements.
Leat	An artificial watercourse or aqueduct dug into the ground of generally very low inclination and used to transfer water from one area to another.
Lithic	Of or pertaining to stone, in particular stone tools.
Lode	A vein of metal ore that fills a space or fissure within a rock or between layers of rock.
Mastaba	A tomb where courtiers and families of monarchs were often buried. Constructed of mud bricks or stone, these rectangular structures are characterised by low sloping walls and a flat roof. Inside a deep burial tunnel descended to the burial chamber.
Nomarch	The governor of an ancient Egyptian nome or province.
Nome	A province or country subdivision.
Nymphaeum	Shrine, monument or grotto dedicated to a minor Greek or Roman female deity or deities that was often associated with springs or other water bodies.
Ostraca	Sherds, small pieces of broken pottery or stone that have been inked or scratched.
Palaeo-channels	The remnants of an inactive river or stream that has been filled or buried by sedimentary material unconnected with the bed load.

Palaeofan   Ancient fan-shaped deposits of sediment caused by the flow of water.

Palaeolithic   A period of prehistory when stone tools were made by humans. The period extends from the earliest known use of the most primitive of stone tools around 2.6 million years ago to the end of the Pleistocene, around 10,000 BP.

Palimpsest   An object made for one purpose but later used for another. The original ancient art of recycling!

Pelusiac   One of the seven ancient distributaries of the Nile.

Playa   A flat-bottomed depression found in desert basins and/or near to coasts in arid/semi-arid regions. Periodically, playas are covered by water that will seep into the groundwater or evaporate, leaving sediment such as salt, sand and mud.

Pleistocene   The geological epoch lasting from 2.5 million years ago to 11,700 BP. The Pleistocene epoch approximately covers a similar timescale as the Palaeolithic, although the former is largely a geological term and the latter archaeological (though this in itself is rather an oversimplistic description).

Qanat   An ancient system of water transportation involving a gently sloping channel from an aquifer or underground water supply to the surface for drinking or for irrigation.

Quaternary   A subdivision of geological time from about 2.5 million years ago to the present. It spans the two most recent epochs – the Pleistocene (from 2.5 million years ago to about 11,700 BP) and the Holocene (from then to the present time).

Rhizocretion   A root system that has been encased in mineral matter.

Sahel   The region between the African Equator and the Saharan region where there is a summer rainy season.

Schist	A medium-grained metamorphic rock with a notable and high degree of foliation.
Sebakh	An Aramaic term to describe decomposed organic matter used for agricultural fertiliser and fuel for heating. Most sebakh consists of ancient, deteriorated mud brick composed of mud mixed with the nitrous compost of hay or stubble.
Shaduf	A hand-operated irrigation device for lifting water from a river, reservoir, well and so on. The shaduf consists of an upright frame on which balances a long pole. At one end of the pole hangs a bucket or some form of container; at the other end is a counterweight.
Speleothem	An overarching term to describe the various forms of mineral deposits in underground caves formed from groundwater, including stalactites and stalagmites.
Stela	An inscribed or carved upright stone slab used for commemorative purposes such as to mark boundaries, to depict tombstones or for religious usage.
Swale	A low tract of often marsh and moist land frequently used to capture channel run off and transport it elsewhere.
Tafla	Beige-coloured desert clay that the ancients used for plaster and mortar in ramps and embankments and for pottery.
Tell	An artificial hill created over hundreds of years by generations of people living and building on the same spot. Gradually over time the level rises, forming a mound, characterised by a flat top and sloping sides (as in a truncated cone).
Tomography	A geophysical technique for creating two- and three-dimensional images of sub-surface structures using electrical sensitivity measurements captured at the surface.

Upcycling   The process of transforming waste material, byproducts and unwanted items into new materials or products.

Waterlain silts/deposits Deposits made up of material washed down rivers or canyons into low-lying areas after sudden storms and deposited to form playas, alluvial fans or perhaps salt pans, depending on the environment.

BIBLIOGRAPHY

Adams, B., 1995. *Ancient Nekhen: Garstang in the City of Hierakonpolis*. Egyptian Studies Association Publication No. 3. New Malden: SIA Publishing.

Alexanian, N., Bebermeier, W. and Blaschta, N., 2011. The Discovery of the Lower Causeway of the Bent Pyramid and the Reconstruction of the Ancient Landscape at Daschur (Egypt). Proceedings of the International Colloquium on Geoarchaeology (Cairo, Egypt, 19–21 September 2010). *Bibliothèque d'Etude, IFAO, le Caire* 169, 296.

Alexanian, N., Bebermeier, W. and Blaschta, D., 2012. Untersuchungen am unteren Aufweg der Knickpyramide in Dahschur. *Mitteilungen des Deutschen Archaologischen Instituts Abteilung Kairo* 68, 1–30.

Alexanian, N., Beberneier, W., Blaschta, D., Ramisch, A., Schütt, B. and Seidlmayer, S. J., 2010. *The Necropolis of Dahshur: Seventh Excavation Report 2009 and 2010*. Berlin: German Archaelogical Institute/Free University of Berlin.

Alexanian, N. and Seidlmayer, S. J., 2002. Residenzne Kropole von Dahshure, Erster Grabungsbericht. *Mitteilungen des Deutschen Archaologischen Instituts Abteilung Kairo* 58, 1–28.

Antoine, J.-C., 2017. Modelling the Nile Agricultural Floodplain in Eleventh and Tenth Century B.C. Middle Egypt: A Study of the P. Wilbour and Other Land Registers. In *The Nile: Natural and Cultural Landscape in Egypt*, edited by H. Willems and J.-M. Dahms. Mainz: Mainz Historical Cultural Sciences, 15–52.

Aslan, A. and Autin, W. J., 1999. Evolution of the Holocene Mississippi River Floodplain, Ferriday, Louisiana: Insights on the Origin of Fine-Grained Floodplains. *Journal of Sedimentary Research* 69, 800–15.

Attia, M. I., 1954. *Deposits in the Nile Valley and the Delta*. Cairo: Geological Survey of Egypt.

Bagnold, R. A., 1935. *Libyan Sands*. London: Travel Book Club.

Bailey, D. M., 1999. Sebakh, Sherds and Survey. *JEA* 85, 211–18.

Baines, J. and Malek, J., 1980. *Cultural Atlas of Ancient Egypt*. Oxford: Phaidon.

Balfour-Paul, J., 2016. *Indigo in the Arab World*. London: Routledge.

Ball, J., 1927. Problems of the Libyan Desert. *The Geographical Journal* 70, 1, 21–38.

　　1932. The "Description de l'Égypte" and the Course of the Nile between Isna and Girga. *Bulletin de l'Institut d'Égypte* 14, 127–39.

　　1939. *Contributions to the Geography of Egypt*. Cairo: Government Press, Bulâq.

Barich, B. E., Lucarini, G., Hamdan, M. A. and Hassan, F. A. (eds.), 2014. *From Lake to Sand: The Archaeology of Farafra Oasis (Egypt)*. Florence: All'Insegna del Giglio.

Beadnell, H. G. L., 1909. Kharga Oasis. Review of *An Egyptian Oasis*. *The Geographical Journal* 34, 5, 561–2. doi:10.2307/1777291.

Behrens-Abouseif, D., 1989. *Islamic Architecture in Cairo*. Leiden: Brill.

Berendsen, H. J. A. and Stouthamer, E., 2001. *Paleogeographic Development of the Rhine-Meuse Delta*. The Netherlands: Van Gorcum.

Bietak, M., 2017. Harbours and Coastal Military Bases in Egypt in the Second Millennium BC. In *The Nile: Natural and Cultural Landscape in Egypt*, edited by H. Willems and J.-M. Dahms. Mainz: Mainz Historical Cultural Sciences, 53–70.

Blackman, A. M. and Fairman, H. W., 1942. The Myth of Horus at Edfu II. C.: The Triumph of Horus over His Enemies: A Sacred Drama. *The Journal of Egyptian Archaeology* 28, 32–8.

Bloxam, E., 1998. The Organisation, Exploitation and Transport of Hard Rock from Cephren's Quarry during the Old Kingdom. Unpublished MA thesis, University College London.

Bloxam, E., 2007. Who Were the Pharoahs' Quarrymen? *Archaeology International* 9, 23–7.

Bloxam, E. and Shaw, I., forthcoming. Feeding the Quarrymen: Environment and Subsistence at the Peripheries of Old Kingdom, Egypt. *Antiquity*.

Boraik, M., Gabolde, L. and Graham, A., 2017. Karnak's Quaysides: Evolution of the Embankments from the Eighteenth Dynasty to the Graeco-Roman Period. In *The Nile: Natural and Cultural Landscape in Egypt*, edited by H. Willems and J.-M. Dahms. Mainz: Mainz Historical Cultural Sciences, 97–144.

Borsch, S. J., 2000. Nile Floods and the Irrigation System in Fifteenth-Century Egypt. *Mamluk Studies Review* 4, 131–46.

Bourrieau, J., 2000. The Second Intermediate Period (c. 1650–1550 BC). In *The Oxford History of Ancient Egypt*, edited by I. Shaw. Oxford: Oxford University Press, 172–206.

Branton, T., 2008. Development of the Memphite Floodplain from Borehole Data. Unpublished dissertation, Cambridge University.

Briois, F., Midant-Reynes, B., Marchand, S., Tristant, Y., Wuttmann, M., De Dapper, M., Lesur, J. and Newton, C. 2012. Neolithic Occupation of an Artesian Spring: KS043 in the Kharga Oasis, Egypt. *Journal of Field Archaeology* 37, 178–91.

Bristow, C. S. and Drake, N., 2006. Shorelines in the Sahara: Geomorphological Evidence for an Enhanced Monsoon from Palaeolake Megachad. *The Holocene* 16, 901–11.

Brook, G., Embabi, N. S., Ashour, M. M., Edwards, R. L., Cheng, H., Cowart, J. B. and Dabous, A. A., 2002. Djara Cave in the Western Desert of Egypt: Morphology and Evidence of Quaternary Climatic Change. *Cave and Karst Science* 29, 57–66.

    2003. Quaternary Environmental Change in the Western Desert of Egypt: Evidence from Cave Speleothems, Spring Tufas and Playa Sediments. *Zeitschrift fur Geomorphologie* N.F. Suppl. 131, 59–87.

Brunton, G. and Engelbach, R. E., 1927. *Gurob*. London: BSAE/ERA.

Bryce, T., 2005. *The Kingdom of the Hittites*. Oxford: Oxford University Press.

Bubenzer, O. and Riemer, H., 2007. Holocene Climatic Change and Human Settlement between the Central Sahara and the Nile Valley: Archaeological and Geomorphological Results. *Geoarchaeology International* 22, 607–20.

Buchez, N. and Midant-Reynes, B., 2007. Le site prédynastique de Kom el-Khilgan (Delta Oriental): Données nouvelles sur les processus d'unification culturelle au IVe millénaire. *BIFAO* 107, 43–70.

Bunbury, J. M., 2016. Geology of the Valley of the Kings. In *Oxford Handbook of the Valley of the Kings*, edited by R. Wilkinson and K. Weeks. Oxford: Oxford University Press, 15–22.

Bunbury, J. M. and Jeffreys, D. J., 2011. Real and Literary Landscapes in Ancient Egypt. *Cambridge Archaeological Journal* 21, 1, 65–76.

Bunbury, J. M. and Malouta, M., 2012. The Geology and Papyrology of Hermopolis and Antinoopolis. In *Landscape Archaeology Conference* (LAC2012). *Journal for Ancient Studies*, Special Volume 3, 119–22.

Bunbury, J. M., Graham, A. and Hunter, M. A., 2008. Stratigraphic Landscape Analysis: Charting the Holocene Movements of the Nile at Karnak through Ancient Egyptian Time. *Geoarchaeology* 23, 351–73.

Bunbury, J. M., Graham, A. and Strutt, K. D., 2009. Kom el-Farahy: A New Kingdom Island in an Evolving Edfu Floodplain. *British Museum Studies in Ancient Egypt and Sudan* 14, 1–23.

Bunbury, J., Hughes, E. and Spencer, N., 2014. Ancient Landscape Reconstruction at Kom Firin. In *Kom Firin II: The Urban Fabric and Landscape*, edited by N. Spencer. British Museum Research Publication, 2 (192). London: The British Museum, 11–16.

Bunbury, J. M., Lutley, K. and Graham, A., 2009. Giza Geomorphological Report. In *Giza Plateau Mapping Project Seasons 2006–2007: Preliminary Report*. Giza Occasional Papers. Boston, MA: Ancient Egypt Research Associates, 158–65.

Bunbury, J., Tavares, A., Pennington, B. and Gonçalves, P., 2017. Development of the Memphite Floodplain. In *The Nile: Natural and Cultural Landscape in Egypt*, edited by H. Willems and J.-M. Dahms. Mainz: Mainz Historical Cultural Sciences, 71–96.

Butzer, K. W., 1959. Some Recent Geological Deposits in the Egyptian Nile Valley. *The Geographical Journal* 125, 75–9.

1976. Early Hydraulic Civilization. In *Egypt: A Study in Cultural Ecology*. Chicago, IL: University of Chicago.

Caton-Thompson, G., 1952. *Kharga Oasis in Prehistory*. London: Athlone Press.

Caton-Thompson, G. and Gardner, E. W., 1932. The Prehistoric Geography of Kharga Oasis. *The Geographical Journal* 80, 369–406.

Çelebi, E., 1938. *Seyahatnâmesi (vol. 10): Misir, Sudan, Habes (1672–1680)*. (*Travelogue (vol. 10): Egypt, Sudan, Ethiopia, 1672–1680*). Istanbul: İkdam Matbaası (Transliterated Ottoman Turkish).

Chaix, L., 1993. The Archaeozoology of Kerma (Sudan). In *Biological Anthropology and the Study of Ancient Egypt*, edited by W. V. Davies and R. Walker. London: British Museum Press, 175–85.

Cohen, J. E., 1995. *How Many People Can the Earth Support?* London: Norton.

Conway, D., 2000. The Climate and Hydrology of the Upper Blue Nile River. *The Geographic Journal*, DOI: 10.1111/j.1475–2000.tb00006.x, 5 July 2005.

Cooper, J., 2014. *The Mediaeval Nile: Route, Navigation, and Landscape in Islamic Egypt*. Cairo: American University in Cairo Press.

Cruz-Uribe, E., 1986. The Hibis Temple Project 1984–85 Field Season, Preliminary Report. *Journal of the American Research Center in Egypt* 23, 157–66.

deMenocal, P., Ortiz, J., Guilderson, T., Adkins, J., Sarnthein, M., Baker, L. and Yarusinsky, M., 2000. Abrupt onset and Termination of the African Humid Period: Rapid Climate Responses to Gradual Insolation Forcing. *Quaternary Science Reviews* 19, 347–61.

Dewald, C. tr. Waterfield, R., 1998. *Herodotus: The Histories*. Oxford: Oxford University Press.

Dorn, A., 2016. The Hydrology of the Valley of the Kings: Weather, Rainfall, Drainage Patterns and Flood Protection in Antiquity. In *Oxford Handbook of the Valley of the Kings*, edited by R. Wilkinson and K. Weeks. Oxford: Oxford University Press, 30–40.

Duckworth, T., 2009. The Development of Islands in the Theban Floodplain. Unpublished dissertation, Cambridge University.

Dufton, D., 2008. Meander Bends of the Nile in the Abydos Region. Unpublished dissertation, Cambridge University.

Dufton, D. and Branton, T., 2009. Climate Change in Early Egypt. *Egyptian Archaeology* 36, 2–3.

Earl, E., 2010. The Lake of Abusir, Northern Egypt. Unpublished dissertation, Cambridge University.

Eiwanger, J., 1992. *Merimde-Benisalame III: Die Funde der jungeren Merimdekultur*. Von Zabern: Mainz.

El-Sanussi, A. and Jones, M., 1997. A Site of the Maadi Culture near the Giza Pyramids. *Mitteilungen des Deutschen Archaologischen Instituts Abteilung Kairo* 53, 241–53.

Embabi, N. S. (ed.), 2004. *The Geomorphology of Egypt: Landforms and Evolution, i: The Nile Valley and the Western Desert*. The Egyptian Geographical Society, Special Publication. Cairo: The Egyptian Geographical Society.

Fairbanks, R. G., 1989. A 17,000 Year Glacio-Eustatic Sea Level Record: Influence of Glacial Melting Rates on the Younger Dryas Event and Deep Ocean Circulation. *Nature* 342, 637–42.

Faulkner, R. O., 1962. *A Concise Dictionary of Middle Egyptian*. Oxford: Griffith Institute.

Fleming, K., Johnston, P., Zwartz, D., Yokoyama, Y., Lambeck, K. and Chappell, J., 1998. Refining the Eustatic Sea-Level Curve since the Last Glacial Maximum Using Far- and Intermediate-Field Sites. *Earth and Planetary Science Letters* 163, 327–42.

Foster, J. L., 2001. *Ancient Egyptian Literature*. Austin, TX: University of Texas Press.

Friedman, R., 2009. Hierakonpolis Locality HK29A: The Predynastic Ceremonial Center Revisited. *Journal of the American Research Center in Egypt* 45, 79–103. www.jstor.org/stable/25735448.

Garcea, E. A. A., 2006. Semi-Permanent Foragers in Semi-Arid Environments of North Africa. In *Sedentism in Non-Agricultural Societies. World Archaeology* 38, 2, 197–219.

Gascoigne, A. L., 2007. The Water Supply of Tinnis: Public Amenities and Private Investments. In *Cities in the Pre-Modern Islamic World: The Urban Impact of Religion, State and Society*, edited by A. K. Bennison and A. L. Gascoigne. London: Routledge, 161–76.

Gasperini, V., 2010. Archaeology and History of the Faiyum in the New Kingdom. PhD dissertation, University of Bologna, in Italian.

Goedicke, H., 1957. The Route of Sinuhe's Flight. *JEA* 43, 77–85.

Goudie, A. and Wilkinson, J., 1977. *The Warm Desert Environment*. Cambridge: Cambridge University Press.

Graham, A., Strutt, K., Toonen, W., Pennington, B., Löwenborg, D., Masson-Berghoff, A., Emery, V., Barker, D., Hunter, M., Lindholm, K.-J. and Johansson, C., 2015. Theban Harbours and Waterscapes Survey, 2015. *Journal of Egyptian Archaeology* 101, 37–49.

Gräzer-Ohara, A., 2012. The Palace of the Mountains on a Re-used Block at Karnak: Amon's *Marou* and/or a Jubilee Complex of Amenhotep III at Malqata. *BIFAO* 112, 191–213, in French.

Groube, L., 1996. The Impact of Diseases upon the Emergence of Agriculture. In *Origins and Spread of Agriculture and Pastoralism in Eurasia*, edited by D. R. Harris. London: Smithsonian Institution Press, 101–29.

Gunn, B. 1927. The Stela of Apries at Mitrahina. *ASAE* 27, 211–37.

Hassan, F. A., 1996. Nile Floods and Political Disorder in Early Egypt. In *Third Millennium BC Climate Change and Old World Collapse*, edited by H. N. Dalfes, G. Kukla and H. Weiss. Berlin: Springer, 1–23.

Haynes, C. V., 1980. Geochronology of Wadi Tushka: Lost Tributary of the Nile. *Science*, 210, 68–71.

Haynes, C. V., Mehringer, P. J. and Zaghloul, S. A., 1979. Pluvial Lakes of North-Western Sudan. *The Geographical Journal* 145, 437–45.

Hendrickx, S., Hugye, D. and Newton, C., 2010. The Walls of El-Kab Wien. In *Cities and Urbanism in Ancient Egypt: Papers from a Workshop in November 2006 at the Austrian Academy of Sciences*. Vienna: Verlag der Österreichischen Akademie der Wissenschaften, 145–70.

Hillier, J. K., Bunbury, J. M. and Graham, A., 2007. Monuments on a Migrating Nile. *Journal of Archaeological Science* 34, 1011–15.

Hobbs, J. J., 1990. *Bedouin Life in the Egyptian Wilderness*. Cairo: American University in Cairo Press.

Hodgkinson, A. K. and Boatright, D., 2009. Cleaning the Kiln Areas Previously Excavated by Brunton and Engelbach in Gridsquares N8–9. In *Report to the SCA on Archaeological Survey Undertaken at Medinet el-Gurob, 1–22 April 2009*, edited by I. Shaw. Unpublished report of SCA available at http://gurob.org.uk/seasons .php, 18–20.

 2010. The Kiln Excavation. In *Report to the SCA on Archaeological Survey and Excavation Undertaken at Medinet el-Gurob, 4–15 April 2010*, edited by I. Shaw. Unpublished report of SCA available at http://gurob.org.uk/seasons.php, 13–16.

Hoffman, M. A., Hamroush, H. A. and Allen, R. O., 1986. The Environmental Evolution of an Early Egyptian Urban Centre: Archaeological and Geochemical Investigations at Hierakonpolis. *Geoarchaeology* 2, 1–13.

Holdaway, S. and Willeke Wendrich, W., 2017. *The Desert Fayum Revisited*. Monumenta Archaeologica 39. Los Angeles, CA: Cotsen Insitute of Archaeology Press.

Hughes, E., 2007. In Search of the Wild Western Branch of the Nile. Unpublished dissertation, Cambridge University.

Ikram, S. and Rossi, C., 2001–. *The North Kharga Oasis Survey: Preliminary Reports*. Cairo: Mitteilungen des Deutschen Archaologischen, Instituts Kairo.

Ikram, S. and Rossi, C., 2004. An Early Dynastic Serekh from the Kharga Oasis. *The Journal of Egyptian Archaeology* 90, 211–15.

Jacquet, J., 1983. *Karnak-Nord V: Le trésor de Thoutmosis Iᵉʳ etude architecturale*. Fouilles de l'Institute Française d'Archéologie Orientale de Caire, 30. Cairo: Institute Française d'Archéologie Orientale.

Jeffreys, D. G., 1985. *The Survey of Memphis I: The Archaeological Report*. London: Egypt Exploration Society.

Jeffreys, D., 2010. *The Survey of Memphis VII: The Hekekyan Papers and Other Sources for the Survey of Memphis*. London: Egypt Exploration Society.

Jeffreys, D. and Bunbury, J. M., 2005. Fieldwork, 2004–05: Memphis, 2004. *Journal of Egyptian Archaeology* 91, 8–12.

Jeffreys, D. and Tavares, A., 1994. The Historic Landscape of Early Dynastic Memphis. *Mitteilungen des Deutschen Archaologischen Instituts Abteilung Kairo* 50, 143–73.

Koopman, A., Kluiving, S., Holdaway, S. and Wendrich, W., 2016. The Effects of Holocene Landscape Changes on the Formation of the Archaeological Record in the Fayum Basin, Egypt. *Geoarchaeology* 31, 17–33.

Kröpelin, S., Verschuren, D., Lézine, A.-M., Eggermont, H., Cocquyt, C., Francus, P., Cazet, J.-P., Fagot, M., Rumes, B., Russell, J. M., Darius, F., Conley, D. J., Schuster, M., von Suchodoletz, H. and Engstrom, D. R., 2008. Climate-Driven Ecosystem Succession in the Sahara: The Past 6000 Years. *Science* 320, 765.

Kuper, R. and Kröpelin, S., 2006. Climate-Controlled Holocene Occupation in the Sahara: Motor of Africa's Evolution. *Science* 313, 803–7.

Lansing, S. J., 2007. *Priests and Programmers: Technologies of Power in the Engineered Landscape of Bali*. Princeton, NJ: Princeton University Press.

Lehner, M., Kamel, M. and Tavares, A., 2009. The Khentkawes Town (KKT). In *Giza Occasional Papers 4*, edited by M. Lehner, M. Kamel and A. Tavares. Boston, MA: Ancient Egypt Research Associates, 9–46.

Levanoni, A., 2008. Water Supply in Medieval Middle Eastern Cities: The Case of Cairo, Al-Masaq. *Journal of the Medieval Mediterranean* 20, 179–205. DOI:10.1080/09503110802283408.

Lichtheim, M., 1973. *Ancient Egyptian Literature I: The Old and Middle Kingdoms*. London: University of California Press.

Lindstadter, J. and Kröpelin, S., 2004. Wadi Bakht Revisited: Holocene Climate Change and Prehistoric Occupation in the Gilf Kebir Region of the Eastern Sahara. *SW Egypt Geoarchaeology* 19, 8, 753–78.

Litherland, P., 2015. *The Western Wadis of the Theban Necropolis*. London: New Kingdom Research Foundation.

Lutley, C. J. and Bunbury, J. M., 2008. The Nile on the Move. *Egyptian Archaeology* 32, 3–5.

Macklin, M. G., Toonen, W. H. J., Woodward, J. C., Williams, M. A. J., Flaux, C., Marriner, N., Nicoll, K., Verstraeten, G., Spencer, N. and Welsby, D., 2015. A New Model of River Dynamics, Hydroclimatic Change and Human Settlement in the Nile Valley Derived from Meta-Analysis of the Holocene Fluvial Archive. *Science* 130, 109–23.

Makaske, B., 1998. *Anastomosing Rivers: Forms, Processes and Sediments*. Netherlands Geographical Studies, 249. Utrecht: Royal Dutch Geographical Society.

Malville, H., Wendorf, F., Mazar, A. and Schild, R., 1998. Megaliths and Neolithic Astronomy in Southern Egypt. *Nature* 292, 488–91.

Maxwell, T. A., Issawi, B. and Haynes, C. V. Jr., 2010. Evidence for Pleistocene Lakes in the Tushka Region, Southern Egypt. *Geology* 38, 1135–8.

McDowell, A., 1999. *Village Life in Ancient Egypt: Laundry Lists and Love Songs*. Oxford: Oxford University Press.

Millet, M. and Masson, A., 2011. *Karnak Settlements*. Los Angeles, CA: UCLA Encyclopedia of Egyptology.

Moeller, N., 2005. The First Intermediate Period: A Time of Famine and Climate Change? *Egypt and the Levant* 15, 153–67.

2006. Tell Edfu Project. www.telledfu.org/annual-reports.

2010. Tell Edfu: Preliminary Report on Seasons 2005–2009. *Journal of the American Research Center in Egypt* 46, 81–111. Retrieved from www.jstor.org/stable/41431571.

Moens, M. and Wetterstrom, W., 1988. The Agricultural Economy of an Old Kingdom Town in Egypt's West Delta: Insights from the Plant Remains. *Journal of Near Eastern Studies* 47, 3, 159–73. Retrieved from www.jstor.org/stable/544958.

Moran, W. L., 1992. *The Amarna Letters*. Baltimore, MD: Johns Hopkins University Press.

Murray, G. W., 1935. *Sons of Ishmael: A Study of the Egyptian Bedouin*. London: Routledge.

1939. The Road to Chephren's Quarries. *The Geographical Journal* 94, 97–111. www .jstor.org/stable/1787245.

1955. Water from the Desert: Some Ancient Egyptian Achievements. *The Geographical Journal* 121, 171–81. www.jstor.org/stable/1791702.

1965. Harkhuf's Third Journey (from his Tomb Wall at Aswan). *The Geographical Journal* 131, 1, 72–5.

Nicholson, P. T., Harrison, J., Ikram, S., Earl, E. and Qin, Y., 2013. Geoarchaeological and Environmental Work at the Sacred Animal Necropolis, North Saqqara, Egypt. *Studia Quaternaria* 30, 83–9.

Parcak, S., 2009. *Satellite Remote Sensing for Archaeology*. London: Routledge.

Parkinson, R., 1991. *Voices from Ancient Egypt*. London: British Museum.

Parsons, P., 2007. *City of the Sharp-Nosed Fish: Greek Lives in Roman Egypt*. Chatham: Phoenix.

Pennington, B. T., Bunbury, J. M. and Hovius, N., 2016. Emergence of Civilization, Changes in Fluvio-Deltaic Style, and Nutrient Redistribution Forced by Holocene Sea-Level Rise. *Geoarchaeology* 31, 3, 194–210.

Petty, B., 2014. *Ahmose: An Egyptian Soldier's Story*. Littleton, CO: Museum Tours Press.

Phillips, R., Holdaway, S. J., Wendrich, W. and Cappers, R., 2012. Mid-Holocene Occupation of Egypt and Global Climatic Change. *Quaternary International* 251, 64–76.

Pokorny, P., Kocar, P., Suvova, Z. and Bezdek, A., 2009. Palaeoecology of Abusir South according to Plant and Animal Remains. In *Abusir XIII: Abusir South 2: Tomb Complex of the Vizier Qar, His Sons Qar Junior and Senedjemib, and Iykai*, edited by M. Barta. Prague: Czech Institute of Egyptology, 29–48.

Polinger Foster, K., Ritner, R. K. and Foster, B. R., 1996. Texts, Storms, and the Thera Eruption. *Journal of Near Eastern Studies* 55, 1–14. www.jstor.org/stable/545376.

Pryer, L., 2011. The Landscape of the Egyptian Middle Kingdom Capital *Itj-Tawi*. Unpublished dissertation, Cambridge University.

Qin, Y., 2009. The Development of the Memphite Floodplain, Egypt. Unpublished dissertation, Cambridge University.

Quibell, J. E., 1900. *Hierakonpolis I*. London: Egyptian Research Account, 4. http:// archive.org/details/hierakonpolis00greegoog.

Redford, S. and Redford, D. B., 1989. Graffiti and Petroglyphs Old and New from the Eastern Desert. *Journal of the American Research Center in Egypt* 26, 3–49.

Ritchie, J. C., Eyles, C. H. and Haynes, C. V., 1985. Sediment and Pollen Evidence for an Early to Mid-Holocene Humid Period in the Eastern Sahara. *Nature* 314, 352–5.

Ritner, R. and Moeller, N., 2014. The Ahmose 'Tempest Stela', Thera and Comparative Chronology. *Journal of Near Eastern Studies* 73, 1, 1–19. Retrieved from www.jstor .org/stable/10.1086/675069.

Robinson, R., El-Baz, F., Ozdogan, M., Ledwith, M., Blanco, D., Oakley, S. and Inzana, J., 2000. Use of Radar Data to Delineate Palaeodrainage Flow Directions in the

Selima Sand Sheet, Eastern Sahara. *Photogrammetric Engineering and Remote Sensing* 66, 745–53.

Rodrigues, D., Abell, P. I. and Kröpelin, S., 2000. Seasonality in the Early Holocene Climate of Northwest Sudan: Interpretation of Etheria Elliptica Shell Isotopic Data. *Global and Planetary Change* 26, 181–7.

Rohde, R., 2006. *Global Warming Art*. www.pinterest.com/mikaidt/climate-change-art/.

Rowland, J. M. and Tassie, G. J., 2014. Prehistoric Sites along the Edge of the Western Nile Delta: Report on the Results of the Imbaba Prehistoric Survey 2013–14. *Journal of Egyptian Archaeology* 100, 56–71.

Said, R., 1962. *The Geology of Egypt*. Amsterdam: Elsevier.

1981. *The Geological Evolution of the River Nile*. New York: Springer Verlag.

1993. *The River Nile: Geology, Hydrology and Utilization*. Oxford: Pergamon Press.

Sampsell, B. M., 2014 (revised edition). *The Geology of Egypt: A Traveller's Handbook*. Cairo: American University in Cairo Press.

Shaw, I. (ed.), 2000. *The Oxford History of Ancient Egypt*. Oxford: Oxford University Press.

2010. Report to the SCA on Archaeological Survey Undertaken at Medinet el-Gurob, 4–15 April 2010, 1–17. www.gurob.org.uk/reports/SCAReport2010.pdf.

Shaw, I., Bloxham, E., Bunbury, J. M., Lee, R., Graham, A. and Darnell, D., 2001. Survey and Excavation at the Gebel el-Asr Gneiss and Quartz Quarries in Lower Nubia (1997–2000). *Antiquity* 75, 33–4.

Shaw, I., Bunbury, J. and Jameson, R., 1999. Emerald Mining in Roman and Byzantine Egypt. *Journal of Roman Archaeology* 12, 203–21.

Sheehan, P., 2015. *Babylon of Egypt: The Archaeology of Old Cairo and the Origins of the City*. Cairo: American University in Cairo Press.

Shepherd, W., 1911. *Historical Atlas*. New York: Henry Holt & Co.

Shirai, N., 2016. The Desert Faiyum at 80: Revisiting a Neolithic Farming Community in Egypt. *Antiquity* 90, 353, 1181–95.

Spence, K. E., 2004. The Three-Dimensional Form of the Amarna House. *Journal of Egyptian Archaeology* 90, 123–52.

Spence, K. E., Rose, P., Bunbury, J., Clapham, A., Collet P., Smith, G. and Soderberg, N., 2009. Fieldwork at Sesebi 2009. *Sudan and Nubia* 13, 38–47.

Spencer, N., 2014. *Kom Firin II: The Urban Fabric and Landscape*. London: The British Museum.

Stanley, D. J., 1988. Subsidence in the North-Eastern Nile Delta: Rapid Rates, Possible Causes, and Consequences. *Science* 240, 497.

Stanley, D. J. and Warne, A. G., 1993. Recent Geological Evolution and Human Impact. *Science* 260, 628–34.

1994. Worldwide Initiation of Holocene Marine Deltas by Deceleration of Sea-Level Rise. *Science* 265, 228–31.

Stanley, J.-D., Krom, M. D., Cliff, R. A. and Woodward, J. C., 2003. Nile Flow Failure at the End of the Old Kingdom, Egypt: Strontium Isotopic and Petrologic Evidence. *Geoarchaeology* 18, 395–402.

Stølum, H.-H., 1997. River Meandering as a Self-Organisation Process. PhD dissertation, University of Cambridge Department of Earth Sciences.

Strabo, 1932. *Geography*, tr. H. Leonard Jones, eds. J. Henderson and G. P. Goold. Loeb Classical Library. London: Harvard University Press.

Subias, E., Fiz, I. and Cuesta, R., 2013. The Middle Nile Valley: Elements in an Approach to the Structuring of the Landscape from the Greco-Roman Era to the Nineteenth Century. *Quaternary International* 312, 27–44, 1–18.

Tallet, G., Garcier, R. J. and Bravard, J.-P., 2011. L'eau disparue d'une micro-oasis: Premiers resultats de la prospection archéologique et geo-archéologique du systeme d'irrigation d'el Deir. In *Les reseaux d'eau courante dans l'antiquité*, edited by C. Abadie-Reynal, S. Provost and P. Vipard. Rennes: Presses Universitaires de Rennes, 173–88.

Tammuz, O., 2005. Mare Clausum? Sailing Seasons in the Mediterranean in Early Antiquity. *Mediterranean Historical Review* 20, 145–62.

Thompson, D., 1998. *Memphis under the Ptolemies*. Princeton, NJ: Princeton University Press.

Thompson, L. G., Mosley-Thompson, E., Davis, M. E., Henderson, K. A., Brecher, H. H., Zagorodnov, V. S., Mashiotta, T. A. Lin, Ping-Nan, Mikhalenko, V. N., Hardy, D. R. and Beer, J., 2002. Kilimanjaro Ice Core Records: Evidence of Holocene Climate Change in Tropical Africa. *Science* 298, 589–93.

Thompson, J., 2015. *Wonderful Things, A History of Egyptology 1: From Antiquity to 1881*. Cairo: American University in Cairo Press.

Toonen, W., 2013. A Holocene Flood Record of the Lower Rhine. Dissertation, Utrecht University Repository. http://igitur-archive.library.uu.nl/dissertations/2013-0923-200637/UUindex.html.

Tristant, Y., 2004. *L'habitat Pre-Dynastique de la vallee du Nil: Vivre sur le rives du Nil aux V et IV Millenaires*. Oxford: Archaeopress.

Twain, M., 1883. *Life on the Mississippi*. Boston: James R. Osgood and Company.

Usai, D., 2005. Early Holocene Seasonal Movements between the Desert and the Nile Valley. Details from the Lithic Industry of some Khartoum Variant and Some Nabta/Kiseiba Sites. *Journal of African Archaeology* 3, 103–15.

Van Neer, W. and Linseele, V., 2016. Interaction between Man and Animals in the Prehistoric Nile Valley. In Science in the Study of Ancient Egypt, edited by S. Zakrzewski, A. Shortland and J. Rowland. New York and London: Routledge, 110–12.

Van Neer, W., Linseele, V. and Friedman, R., 2002. Animal Burials and Food Offerings at the Elite Cemetery HK6 of Hierakonpolis. In *Egypt at its Origins: Studies in Memory of Barbara Adams*, edited by S. Hendrickx, R. F. Friedman, K. M. Cialowicz and M. Chlodnicki, M. Orientalia Lovaniensia Analecta 138. Leuven: Peeters, 67–130.

2009. Special Animals from a Special Place? The Fauna from HK29A at Predynastic Hierakonpolis. *Journal of the American Research Center in Egypt* 45, 105–36.

Van Pelt, P., 2013. Revising Egypto-Nubian Relations in New Kingdom Lower Nubia: From Egyptianization to Cultural Entanglement. *Cambridge Archaeological Journal* 23, 3, 523–50.

Verstraeten, G., Mohamed, I., Notebaert, B. and Willems, H., 2017. The Dynamic Nature of the Transition from the Nile Floodplain to the Desert in Central Egypt since the Mid-Holocene. In *The Nile: Natural and Cultural Landscape in Egypt*, edited by H. Willems and J.-M. Dahms. Mainz: Mainz Historical Cultural Sciences, 239–54.

Watson, R. T., Zinyowera, M. C. and Moss, R. H. (eds.), 1997. *The Regional Impacts of Climate Change: An Assessment of Vulnerability*. Cambridge: Cambridge University Press.

Weerts, H., 1996. Complex Confining Layers: Architecture and Hydraulic Properties of Holocene and Late Weichselian Deposits in the Fluvial Rhine-Meuse Delta. PhD thesis, University of Utrecht, Netherlands Geographical Studies, 213.

Weinsten, J., 1971–2. A Foundation Deposit Tablet from Hierakonpolis. *JARCE* 9, 133–5.

Welsby, D. A., 2001. *Life on the Desert Edge: Seven Thousand Years of Settlement in the Northern Dongola Reach, Sudan.* SARS Monograph, No. 7, London. Oxford: BAR Int. Ser. 980.

Welsby, D., 2013. Reach-Scale River Dynamics Moderate the Impact of Rapid Holocene Climate Change on Floodwater Farming in the Desert Nile. *Geology* 41, 695–8.

Wendorf, F. and The Members of the Combined Prehistoric Expedition, 1977. Late Pleistocene and Recent Climatic Changes in the Egyptian Sahara. *The Geographical Journal*, 143, 211–34. www.jstor.org/.

Wendorf, F. and Schild, R., 1998. Nabta Playa and Its Role in Northeastern African Prehistory. *Journal of Anthropological Archaeology* 17, 97–123.

Wenke, R. J., 1988. Kom El-Hisn: Excavation of and Old Kingdom Settlement in the Egyptian Delta. *JARCE* 25, 5–34.

Willcocks, W., 1889. *Egyptian Irrigation.* London: E. & F. N. Spon.

1904. *The Nile in 1904.* London. E. & F. N. Spon.

Wilson, P., 2006. *The Survey of Saïs (Sa el-Hagar), 1997–2002.* Excavation Memoirs. Egypt Exploration Society. London: Oxbow Books.

Wilson, P. and Gilbert, G., 2003. The Prehistoric Period at Sais (Sa el Hagar). *Archéo-Nil* 13, 65–72.

Winlock, H. E., 1910, The Egyptian Expedition. *The Metropolitan Museum of Art Bulletin* 5, 221–8.

Woodward, J. C., Macklin, M. G., Krom, M. D. and Williams, A. J., 2007. The Nile: Evolution, Quarternary River Environments and Material Fluxes. In *Large Rivers, Geomorphology and Management*, edited by A. Gupta. London: Wiley, 261–92.

Woodward, J. C., Macklin, M. G. and Welsby, D., 2001. The Holocene Fluvial Sedimentary Record and Alluvial Geoarchaeology in the Nile Valley of Northern Sudan. In *River Basin Sediment Systems: Archives of Environmental Change*, edited by D. Maddy, M. G. Macklin and J. C. Woodward. Amsterdam: AA Balkema, 327–55.

INDEX

Notes: Page numbers in *italics* denotes figures and **bold** denotes tables.